Understanding Psychological Testing in Children

A GUIDE FOR HEALTH PROFESSIONALS

Understanding Psychological Testing in Children

A GUIDE FOR HEALTH PROFESSIONALS

Stewart Gabel, M.D.
New York Hospital–Cornell Medical Center
White Plains, New York

Gerald D. Oster, Ph.D.
Regional Institute for Children and Adolescents (RICA)
Rockville, Maryland

Steven M. Butnik, Ph.D.
Independent Practice
Richmond, Virginia

PLENUM MEDICAL BOOK COMPANY
New York and London

Library of Congress Cataloging in Publication Data

Gabel, Stewart, 1943–
    Understanding psychological testing in children.

    Includes bibliographies and index.
    1. Psychological tests for children. I. Oster, Gerald D. II. Butnik, Steven M. III. Title.
    [DNLM: 1. Psychological Tests—in infancy & childhood. WS 105.5.E8 G112u]
    RJ503.5.G33   1986   155.4   86-15104
    ISBN 0-306-42244-1

© 1986 Plenum Publishing Corporation
233 Spring Street, New York, N.Y. 10013

Plenum Medical Book Company is an imprint of Plenum Publishing Corporation

Printed in the United States of America

Preface

There is a considerable amount of interest within pediatrics and primary health care that is currently being directed toward the behavioral and emotional problems of childhood. Traditionally, these areas have been emphasized by child psychiatrists, child psychologists, and psychiatric social workers. Now, however, the detection and, in some cases, the assessment and treatment of children with these types of disturbances fall within the province of primary child health care professionals. Even when the child psychiatrist or child psychologist provides the primary mental health treatment for the child, specialists such as pediatricians, family physicians, pediatric nurses, pediatric nurse practitioners, and speech therapists remain instrumental in support of the ongoing psychotherapeutic process as providers of some other aspect of total health care to the child and family.

For these pediatricians, family physicians, and other nonpsychologist primary health care providers, it is essential to acquire an understanding and effective working knowledge of important psychological information and concepts to utilize within their own framework and professional responsibilities. In order that this may be accomplished, these professionals with limited backgrounds in psychology must better understand how psychologists themselves assess children and how they derive the conclusions reflected in the statements and reports that are shared with members of their own and other disciplines. In short, nonpsychologists must become substantially more familiar with psychological assessment, particularly with psychological testing and the subsequent reporting of results. They need to be able to assimilate and evaluate the strengths, weaknesses, presumptions, language, and goals of testing and be able to comprehend the concepts and jargon of psychologists.

However, communicating the results of psychological testing is beset with many problems. In order to provide accurate interpretation of testing, the psychologist must rely on appropriate normative data, feel confident regarding the reliability and validity of specific tests, consider the developmental level of the child, and possess sound clinical judgment. This information must then be transmitted effectively to all members of the medical evaluation team and to parents and others involved in the referral and planning process. Finally, the feedback, whether written or verbal, must be presented in such a manner as to minimize the possibility of improper conclusions and misinterpretation of data, and at the same time be relevant and useful.

In creating an approach to assessment and evaluation, psychologists have relied on a broad array of tests that attempt to tap various aspects of psychological functioning. These include screening forms, cognitive instruments, personality inventories, educational tests, and psychosocial scales. These measures delineate levels of intellectual functioning, perceptual skills, language development, social and emotional adaptation, judgment in interpersonal situations, acquired knowledge, and motor dexterity. The range of these tests is enormous.

This book offers an explanatory guide to the most widely used psychological tests in children. Although not meant to be comprehensive, it attempts to provide a meaningful overview and evaluation of numerous specific instruments as a useful tool for child health care professionals involved in the evaluation and treatment of children.

This book is intended to aid the nonpsychologist in understanding psychological testing through: (1) clarifying the needs of child health care providers with regard to psychological evaluations; (2) explaining the concepts and assumptions of psychological testing in language which is clear and useful to those in other professions; (3) discussing the findings, utility, and role of specific tests referred to on written reports or during verbal feedback; and (4) detailing the relationship between psychological testing and medical and neurological evaluations. Finally, guidelines will be provided for nonpsychologists in discussing with parents the results of psychological tests on children.

We have endeavored to create a concise, practical, and clinically oriented guide. Numerous case illustrations will be presented. While the main readership is planned to be child health care providers such as pediatricians and family physicians, other professionals such as clinical social workers and psychiatric nurses, who are also actively involved with psychologically disturbed children, may find the book useful. Child psychologists may also find this book helpful by enlarging their own perspectives on what physicians and other professionals find important and meaningful in the reports that they receive from psychologists.

STEWART GABEL, M.D.
GERALD D. OSTER, Ph.D
STEVEN M. BUTNIK, Ph.D

Contents

1 The Nature of Psychological Testing   1

2 The Child Health Care Professional's Relationship to Psychological Testing   9

3 The Referral for Psychological Testing   19

4 The Psychological Report   25

5 Behavior Rating Scales   35

   Conners Teacher and Parent Rating Forms   36
   Child Behavior Checklist   37
   Behavior Problem Checklist   46

6 Screening Instruments   49

   Denver Developmental Screening Test (DDST)   50
   Developmental Screening Inventory (DSI), including the Gesell
   Scales of Infant Development   54
   Goodenough-Harris Drawing Test (Draw-A-Person Test)   55
   Peabody Picture Vocabulary Test—Revised   59
   Slosson Intelligence Test   61

7   Cognitive Measures   65

Bayley Scales of Infant Development   66
Stanford-Binet Intelligence Scale   69
Wechsler Scales (WISC-R, WPPSI)   75
McCarthy Scales of Children's Abilities   82
Kaufman Assessment Battery for Children   84
Leiter International Performance Scale   89

8   Educational and Perceptual Testing   93

Illinois Test of Psycholinguistic Abilities (ITPA)   94
Peabody Individual Achievement Test (PIAT)   96
Wide Range Achievement Test (WRAT)   99
Bender Visual-Motor Gestalt Test   101
Developmental Test of Visual Motor Integration   105

9   Neuropsychological Tests   109

Halstead-Reitan Test Battery   110
Luria Nebraska Neuropsychological Test Battery   117

10   Tests of Social/Adaptive Skills   121

American Association on Mental Deficiency Scale
(AAMD)   122
Vineland Social Maturity Scale and Vineland Adaptive Behavior Scales   124

11   Personality Inventories and Projective Measures   129

House-Tree-Person   130
Sentence Completion Tests   137
Thematic Apperception Test (TAT) and Children's Apperception Test (CAT)   139
Rorschach Technique   143
Minnesota Multiphasic Personality Inventory (MMPI)   146

12   The Relationship between Psychological Test Results and Medical and Neurological Problems   153

13   The Child Health Profession Talks to Parents: The Informing Interview   165

Index   181

Chapter 1

The Nature of Psychological Testing

CASE ILLUSTRATIONS

The mother of Josh L. had suspected problems for some time; however, it was not until Josh's fourth-grade teacher called that Mrs. L. decided to begin to look for more definite answers. Josh's inattentiveness had increased after Christmas vacation and he had begun to act in a hostile manner toward children who had been his friends. His continuing disinterest in school was reflected in incompleted homework assignments with concomitant declining grades. Mrs. L. had discussed her concern in the past with her pediatrician, but no intervention was attempted. With these new developments, Mrs. L. and the pediatrician decided to have a private psychologist perform a thorough evaluation of Joshua. The pediatrician provided Mrs. L. with the name of a clinical child psychologist with whom he had worked in the past. She then called the psychologist, who gathered the historical antecedents of the problem from discussion with Mrs. L., thus beginning the assessment process. As a result of this conversation, it was decided that they schedule a testing session to delineate Josh's problem areas further. The psychologist forwarded to Mr. and Mrs. L. behavioral rating scales and also sent a version of the scale to Josh's teacher. On the day of the testing, Mr. and Mrs. L. provided additional information regarding early development, family history, and current family interaction. With this information, the psychologist was ready to introduce himself to Josh and begin the actual testing process.

Damon B., aged 8, was referred for psychological evaluation by a family physician who had found no physical reasons for complaints of severe headaches. Parental descriptions of his behavior portrayed Damon as being unmanageable both at home and at school. His schoolwork seemed to be declining and he was described as moody, overly active, and involved in many fights. After initial history taking was completed, a recommendation for testing was made based on concerns regarding general intellectual status, possible need for special educational remediation, the possibility of information-processing problems (an audiologist's report suggested the possibility of a slight auditory processing deficit), and the extent of generalized anxiety interfering with the learning process.

A psychological evaluation of Mathew F., aged 12, was requested by the school from which he had been expelled for fighting. He was described as overly active and academically inconsistent, with grades going from As to Ds. He had few friends and continually misbehaved and fought in the schoolyard. He was also suspected of having set several fires in church. A medical report indicated that he had been in good health all of his life and had no recent medical problems. He had begun persistent bedwetting upon entering school, and a medical evaluation at that time had been negative. This problem persisted, although on an irregular basis, at the time of the evaluation. Testing was required for proper psychological evaluation and treatment of his several problem areas.

Although the problems addressed in the above case illustrations are only a fraction of the myriad of disorders frequently confronted by a clinical psychologist, the vignettes are examples of the need for assessment procedures. The commonality these and other cases share involves perplexing behaviors, emotional reactions, and learning problems that require further examination and explanation to help the child and others who are in positions of responsibility for the child's growth and development. Within this information-gathering process, the need arises for an objective and thorough understanding of the child's strengths and weaknesses, as well as insight into how these abilities might become manifest in the child's everyday life. Thus the need becomes paramount for devices that measure those characteristics of the child that pertain to cognitive and emotional growth and expressions of behavior. The major function of these devices (i.e., psychological tests) is to define the causes and breadth of the disturbance in order to help in formulating a desirable treatment intervention.

Psychological tests have become the major source of objective and substantive information concerning personal skills and performances. Testing in a narrow sense refers to the technical process of administering a psychologically relevant instrument. In a broader sense, testing refers to the more complex process of integrating and understanding the results of all components of the formal tests and test battery.[1] When this process of testing is added to the other aspects of the evaluation such as the developmental history, interviews with the child, parents, and teachers, and observations of the child's behavior, it is more aptly described as the assessment process. This book addresses mainly that segment of this assessment process that relies on the actual tests and interpretation of tests that psychologists use in gaining the needed information in order to clarify the nature and extent of the problem behaviors.

Keeping in mind the biological and social aspects of the child's development, which are the essential elements of the assessment process, the psychologist attempts to delineate the child's unique patterns of strengths and weaknesses in academics, intelligence, and personality development. Identifying and understanding these patterns allow for a clear response to the referral question and for the development of a practical set of treatment or intervention strategies. In order to accomplish these goals, standardized tests have been constructed to gauge a wide variety of psychological characteristics.

Psychological tests gain their meaning through comparisons with stated criteria, or what are generally termed norms or normative values.[2] These norms are judged either by the child's personal performance on a test or by comparison of that child's performance with that of a group comprised of similar children who have taken the same tests in a parallel situation. An example of using a child's own results as the criterion is when treatment is attempted after initial baseline information has been obtained on a test and then the effectiveness of remediation is later measured by administering the same test to the child. It might also be important to compare the child's test results with those obtained from samples of children of the same age. For instance, does a 7-year-old girl exhibit the same ability on a measure of perceptual maturation as same-aged peers? The most common use of group norm comparisons is probably seen on intelligence tests, wherein the derived IQ is equated to scores of children who have attempted to complete the same set of tasks.[3]

Occasionally, a child's performance on a test is judged against other criteria such as chronological age or grade level. Thus, scores might also be expressed in the form of mental age or in terms of school placement. Interpreting the scores in this manner may, for example, allow the clinician to recommend that parents or teachers adopt a less complex approach to the child if the child's functioning is on a lower developmental level.[2]

The focus of psychological testing remains on the objectivity that it lends in forming a clearer diagnosis and understanding of the referred child's behavior, development, and overall learning abilities and accomplishments. Although previous evaluations may have included a thorough history and set of observations to produce many clinical hypotheses, these may be distorted through omissions or subjective biases. Psychological tests offer the physician or any other health professional who is investigating the source of a child's problems a wealth of information which is more likely to be free from these influences and biases.[3]

However, no psychological or educational test is totally free of error. A degree of inaccuracy is always present when attempts are made to measure abilities or traits.[4] Errors can be systematic or random. Some tests tend to produce systematically high or low results which will distort the child's actual abilities or traits. Other tests may be unreliable in that results may fluctuate dramatically from day to day or may change in the hands of different examiners. Unfortunately, tests do differ greatly in their degree of accuracy. When salient decisions are being made on the basis of unreliable instruments, those decisions may also be in error. Additionally, when psychological tests are selected, a thorough consideration of the rationale for using that particular test should be made. If test administrators fail to consider their purposes for selecting a test, the test may be used inappropriately. In a similar manner, if test administrators fail to consider the assumptions underlying a specific test, the results can lead to overgeneralizations (e.g., using the Peabody Picture Vocabulary Test[5] as a test of generalized intelligence).

The decision as to which tests to administer to a child varies according to referral questions, the referral source and agency involved, time constraints, and other situational factors. Within the overall assessment process, tests are viewed as one method of obtaining the most relevant data in the shortest amount of time. Before the actual testing session begins, an awareness of the problem or referral question is most important.[3] Although a general request might come through on a form, it is often too vague to communicate the needed information. Thus, the examiner sometimes must return to the referral source to gain additional insight into what is being asked.

A battery of tests is typically chosen in order to allow the child the opportunity to express various abilities and levels of functioning. No individual test can answer all questions posed to yield a definitive impression and no test alone can differentiate among all abilities, some of which may be obscured by the presenting disturbance.

Most psychologists use a set of tests with which they have become comfortable over time and which has provided them with standardized norms in certain instances and with a personal baseline for normal versus abnormal performance in other cases. This test battery has been found to be useful by the psychologist in assessing most clinical problems, although truly capable psychologists are constantly receptive to the possibility that new tests or revised normative data on already existing tests will enhance their knowledge of and usefulness to the child and his or her caretakers.

The specific tests of a battery usually include a variety intended to evaluate different aspects of a child's functioning. Intelligence tests for different age groups (e.g., the Bayley Scales of Infant Development,[6] the Wechsler Intelligence Scale for Children-Revised[7]) and measures used for children with handicapping conditions whose maximum abilities may not be accurately detailed by the more common methods are almost always included.[8] Also included in a standard test battery are measures assessing educational abilities and achievement. These tests of spelling, reading, language development, and arithmetic are included to specify the strengths and weaknesses of a child as well as discrepancies between potential and achievement.

Testing can also be used to delineate clinical problems such as signs of brain dysfunction, personality disorder, and severe emotional disturbance, and test batteries often include particular tests to address these sorts of problems.[9] In the past, results of perceptual motor tests such as the Bender Visual-Motor Gestalt Test[10] were used as indicators of brain impairment or *organicity*.[11] However, the realization of the complexity between brain and behavior has initiated a movement in psychology toward the use of extended neuropsychological batteries (e.g., the Halstead-Reitan[12]) to provide a clearer picture of deficits in abilities relating to motor coordination, memory, attention, and the like.[13] Tests which provide the psychologist with information regarding the child's inner experiences and emotional conflicts (e.g., the Children's Apperception Test[14]) aid in demonstrating how these perceptions of the child's environment might hinder and intrude on his or her growth and development. For example, a child might be especially sensitive to events in his or her personal world (e.g., parents divorcing) or to situational events in the external world (e.g., war) that might impact on academic and/or social functioning. Such tests as the Rorschach[15] may be included in the battery of the psychologist to evaluate the possibility of a severe emotional disturbance such as a psychosis. Use of the Rorschach also provides rich information concerning the child's perceptual style and how it might relate to the child's personality organization.

Not only is it important to have a full appreciation of the attributes and limitations of psychological tests; it is also important to understand that the psychologist himself or herself is a mediating variable in the assessment process. The competent examiner should have proper training and experience in addition to certain key personal qualities. Appropriate training includes a graduate degree in an applied area of psychology (clinical psychology, counseling, or school psychology) with specific courses on test theory and test construction and courses on statistics and measurement. Also essential in this preparation are supervised field placements and clinical internships in which emphasis is placed on exposure to a wide variety of clinical populations with instruction and tutelage by experienced clinicians. For psychologists involved in the testing of children, courses on child development are necessary prerequisites and supervised clinical experiences should focus on children from infancy through adolescence. Throughout the United States, psychologists are frequently licensed and/or certified through their particular state boards of psychology with reference to these kinds of educational and training requirements to ensure that high standards of the profession are met.

Beyond the academic and experiential training, the psychologist involved in assessing and testing children must have sufficient personal social skill to be able to establish rapport with the most anxious and difficult child. Further, the trained examiner must be able to extract the child's highest level of motivation and cooperation with the least departure from standard test administration procedures. This skill involves knowing when to be patient, encouraging, or demanding in response to the child's test-taking behaviors. These personal qualifications are important not only for the psychologist–child relationship but also in relation to the psychologist and the referral source, between whom much important communication transpires that will have a major influence on the welfare of the child. Several of these points are emphasized further in subsequent chapters.

References

1. Cronbach LJ: *Essentials of Psychological Testing*, ed 3. New York, Harper International Edition, 1970.
2. Anastasi A: *Psychological Testing*, ed 5. New York, Macmillan, 1982.

3. Berger M: Psychological testing, in Rutter M and Hersov L (eds): *Child and Adolescent Psychiatry: Modern approaches.* London: Blackwell Scientific Publications, 1976.

4. Stanley JC: Reliability, in Thorndike RL (ed): *Educational Measurement,* ed 2. Washington, DC: American Council on Education, 1971.

5. Dunn LM, Dunn LM: *Peabody Picture Vocabulary Test—Revised.* Circle Pines, Minnesota, American Guidance Services, 1981.

6. Bayley N: *Bayley Scales of Infant Development: Birth to Two Years.* New York, Psychological Corporation, 1969.

7. Wechsler D: *Manual for the Wechsler Intelligence Scale for Children—Revised.* New York, Psychological Corporation, 1974.

8. Sattler JM: *Assessment of Children's Intelligence and Special Abilities,* ed 2., Boston, Allyn & Bacon, 1982.

9. Garfield SL: *Clinical Psychology.* Chicago, Aldine, 1974.

10. Bender L: *A Visual Motor Gestalt Test and its Clinical Use.* New York, The American Orthopsychiatric Association, 1938.

11. Herbert M: *Emotional Problems of Development in Children.* London, Academic Press, 1974.

12. Reitan RM: Methodological problems in clinical neuropsychology, in Reitan RM, and Davison LA (eds): *Clinical Neuropsychology: Current status and applications.* Washington, DC: Winston, 1974.

13. Davison LA: Introduction, in Reitan RM, and Davison LA (eds): *Clinical Neuropsychology: Current status and applications.* Washington, DC: Winston, 1974.

14. Bellak L: *The TAT, CAT and SAT in Clinical Use,* ed 3. New York, Grune & Stratton, 1975.

15. Rorschach H: *Psychodiagnostics.* Berne, Huber, 1942.

Chapter 2

The Child Health Care Professional's Relationship to Psychological Testing

Exactly how much physicians and other child health care professionals must know about psychological testing and psychological tests depends on the role that the particular health care provider serves in providing services to children with learning and behavior problems. For physicians and other health care providers, this role has expanded considerably in the recent past.[1]

This chapter will discuss and illustrate a variety of roles that primary care physicians play in providing health care to children that might lead the provider himself or herself to perform psychological tests, refer a child with academic or behavior problems for formal testing by a psychologist, or be required to explain the results of psychological testing done elsewhere to parents or to the child prior to treatment.

The next chapter will discuss the role of the psychologist from the physician's point of view, as that role pertains to performing the tests, writing reports, and communicating findings to the physician (or other child health care provider). The issue of how much the physician must know about psychological testing in order to feel comfortable in understanding the test results and communicating the results to his or her patients will also be mentioned then.

The Role of the Health Care Provider in Working with Children Who Have Learning or Behavior Problems

Primary care physicians may have varying degrees of responsibility in the care of children with actual or potential psychological disorders. One role involves attempting to prevent the occurrence of certain psychological and mental handicaps (e.g., by screening for phenylketonuria in newborns). Another role involves attempting to detect certain mental disorders in their early or asymptomatic stages (e.g., screening for developmental delays). A third role involves treating common behavior problems of a mild, developmental, or situationally induced nature (e.g., temper tantrums in a toddler, school refusal in a 6-year-old, relatively uncomplicated grief reactions in a normal youngster who has recently lost a parent through accident or illness). A fourth role involves coordination and collaboration with primary mental health care providers such as clinical child psychologists or child psychiatrists or with educators in the treatment of children with more severe emotional or behavioral disorders. An example of the latter would be treating the child having an attention deficit disorder with hyperactivity when the physician prescribes and supervises the use of stimulant medication and when the teacher or special education consultant designs behavioral programs or special education classes.

Almost all of these roles may require the physician's involvement with the child psychologist and/or with psychological testing at some point.

The Physician Performing a Psychological Test

CASE ILLUSTRATION 1

Carla D. is 2 years and 4 months old and white; she has been followed by the same pediatrician since birth. She has had no major medical problems and, except for routine health supervision, has been seen by her physician on only a few occasions. Her parents have been concerned about her development since she was about 9 to 12 months of age. She said "Mama," "Dada," and other simple *consonant and vowel sounds later than her two older siblings; she did not speak single words which were understandable to her parents until 15 months of age; and currently she can say several single words but no two-word phrases.* Her hearing has not been questioned, even during the few episodes of otitis media that she has had. She has also been rather slow in her ability to stack blocks and manipulate objects. She has been described as having little interest in books and stories, but overall she seems to be a happy child who relates well, is performing normally for her age in dressing and undressing skills, and is almost toilet-trained for bowel and bladder except for frequent nighttime episodes of bed wetting. Her gross motor development has been normal since birth; she currently runs well, walks up steps, can balance briefly on each foot, can kick a ball, and can throw it overhand.

Carla's growth parameters have been within normal limits. There is no history in the family of developmental delays or mental retardation. Previous assessments at appropriate intervals with a suitable screening test—in this case the Denver Developmental Screening Test (DDST)[2,3]—have all been unremarkable. Screening for hearing problems with various noise makers and by questions about the child's language and response to sounds and questions in the home environment have shown no abnormalities.[4,5]

At this point, however, with the child continuing to show delays in language and possibly in other areas, another DDST was performed. The results were now abnormal, with delays in the language area and in the fine motor/adaptive area. Carla was therefore referred to an audiologist for an assessment of hearing, which was evaluated by a play conditioning procedure. No abnormalities were found. She was also referred to a psychologist for further testing.

Using various psychological tests, including the Bayley Scales of Infant Development, the Cattell Infant Intelligence Scale, and the Stanford-Binet Intelligence Scale, the psychologist found that overall Carla functioned developmentally at a level several months below her chronological age and that she had particularly poor expressive language abilities. Receptive language skills were found to be somewhat better. She was referred to a preschool developmental stimulation program and later to speech and language therapy. A follow-up showed good school adjustment; grades were average.

This case is intended to illustrate the physician's careful following of children with suspected developmental delays and his or her use of screening tests to identify children who should be referred for more in-depth testing. Screening for developmental problems is now an accepted part of the child health care provider's role. The authors feel that the use of standardized screening devices (see Chapter 6) is far preferable to an informal question and observation approach. Using standardized instruments is not difficult, is relatively rapid, can be done by the physician, nurse, or health aide, and provides an ongoing, longitudinal profile of the child's developmental progress. Results are objective, can be compared with other psychological measures, and provide a picture of the child developmentally that can be communicated to other health care providers or to the psychologist. Screening tests such as the DDST or the Developmental Screening Inventory (see Chapter 6) require considerable familiarity to insure their proper application, but, unlike most psychological tests to be discussed in this book, they are intended for use by nonpsychologists as a first-line assessment device.

The Physician Referring a Child with Learning or Behavior Problems for Psychological Testing

CASE ILLUSTRATION 2

John E. is 7½ years old and a second-grader; he has been followed by his current pediatrician for two years. He is the middle child with an older sister aged 9 and a younger brother aged 5½. John was premature and had respiratory distress syndrome at birth, spent four weeks in the hospital after birth (six days on a respirator), and has generally been slower than his siblings developmentally. With hard work, however, he did reasonably well in first grade. He has had no significant behavior problems in school, although at times he seems to lack confidence and to exhibit excessive shyness, according to previous teachers. At home recently his usually reserved manner has been replaced by angry outbursts, aggressiveness, and oppositional behavior. The teacher at school has reported no behavior problems or behavioral changes in that setting.

John was seen by his pediatrician for a more detailed assessment of the behavioral change at home. He was interviewed; his drawings of a person were reviewed for developmental level and emotional indicators (see Chapters 6 and 11); he was asked to perform a variety of developmentally appropriate tasks; and he was also assessed during a brief play session. A physical examination, including an evaluation of neurodevelopmental functioning, was performed.[6] The parents were both interviewed for relevant developmental, behavioral, and family history.

As a result of the assessment, the pediatrician felt that John's behavior at home was probably deteriorating because of increasing frustration at school and difficulty in keeping up with his chronological age peers academically. A treatment plan was formulated in which the pediatrician would work with John in play and discussion sessions and with his parents in management and guidance sessions over the course of about six weeks. These visits were intended to help John and his family understand his behavior problems and deal with them more effectively in the home and school environments.

As an additional part of the treatment plan, the pediatrician (with John's and his parents' consent) contacted the school and discussed John's problem with his teacher. Since the pediatrician was planning to provide therapy for John and his family. he felt that more in-depth psychological testing would be helpful as a guide in working with John behaviorally and also as an aid in understanding his overall intellectual ability and development. This too was discussed with the teacher. The latter agreed that testing, especially for a possible learning disability that she was beginning to suspect, might be helpful for educational purposes and was even more clearly indicated now that behavior problems had arisen.

Psychological testing was completed through a referral by the pediatrician to a psychologist working privately in the area (it might also have been done through a psychologist working in the school setting). The results of the psychological testing derived from a test battery that included the Wechsler Intelligence Scale for Children—Revised (WISC–R), the Draw-A-Person Test, the Bender Visual-Motor Gestalt Test, Family Drawings, the Children's Apperception Test and the Illinois Test of Psycholinguistic Abilities (see appropriate chapters) did in fact indicate that John had a specific learning disability in the visual-motor area. The projective tests, drawings, and additional interviewing by the psychologist supported the pediatrician's assessment of the cause of the recent behavioral change as being secondary to academic frustration.

These results provided additional support and further insights to the pediatrician later in working with John and his family. The psychological test results indicated that John's behavior problems were largely of an adjustment nature and were not currently very severe. This appeared to confirm the pediatrician's view that he, a primary health care clinician, could work successfully with John. Later, after appropriate additional conferences with school personnel, the test results were used to support John's receiving additional academic resource help in the school environment.

CASE ILLUSTRATION 3

Alan W. is 6 years and 2 months old and has been followed by his current pediatrician for four years. Since the child was a toddler, the parents have complained that he was overactive, impulsive, and prone to mischief. Prenatal, perinatal, and postnatal medical histories were unremarkable. Growth and developmental milestones have been within normal limits. Family history revealed that a maternal uncle was "hyperactive" as a child, truant, and a high-school dropout as an adolescent.

Alan's behavior problems were managed relatively easily by his parents in consultation with the pediatrician during the preschool years. Since school entry, however, behavior problems that have included aggression, hyperactivity, impulsivity, and immaturity have become worse in school and home settings. Academic work has always been average to slightly above average.

Alan's parents have brought him to his pediatrician on the teacher's recommendation. The latter wonders if medication would help "slow him down" and help him "pay attention" better. The pediatrician's previous contacts with Alan and his family have led him to believe that Alan may indeed have an attention deficit disorder with hyperactivity. Behavioral approaches alone were quite successful in helping Alan and his family previously, but it now appears that the school setting and increasing academic demands have pressed Alan's ability to cope beyond their limits.

The pediatrician's impression is that the teacher may very well be suggesting an appropriate additional treatment modality for Alan. The pediatrician had previously evaluated Alan by careful history, interview and play session, and physical examination with attention to minor congenital anomalies and neurodevelopmental functioning.[7] Prior to instituting medication, he decides to evaluate hyperactivity and behavioral problems in a more standardized manner by the use of the Conners parent and teacher rating scales.[8,9,10] Alan's ratings on the scales can now be used as a baseline against which further ratings can be obtained if and when medication is instituted. In this manner treatment effects can be measured over time.

Alan's mother and teacher completed the Conners parent and teacher rating Forms, and Alan did indeed score high on the Hyperactivity scale on both forms, although relatively higher on the teacher's than on the parent's form. At this point it was clear that a trial of stimulant medication was indicated. The pediatrician also was concerned that although Alan's grades were average, a previously unsuspected learning disability might be missed. He suspected this because of research suggesting that large numbers of children with attentional deficits do have specific learning disabilities. He therefore recommended further psychological and educational testing after speaking with the teacher, who felt this might be valuable.

Psychological testing was done prior to starting medication. A test battery similar to that of the previous illustration was employed. Results showed a Full Scale IQ on the WISC—R that was well above average (110), a significant discrepancy between Verbal and Performance scales on the same test (Verbal IQ 95, Performance IQ

128) and low subscale scores on Arithmetic, Coding, and Digit Span (the freedom from distractibility factor), reflecting attentional deficits. Auditory processing problems were also noted on the Illinois Test of Psycholinguistic Abilities (ITPA). On the basis of these results, it was apparent that Alan's "average" school performance reflected learning problems in light of his above-average potential. These learning difficulties were the result of attentional deficits and auditory processing problems. He had fortunately been able to keep up academically with his peers of average abilities thus far.

Alan's additional assessment by the psychologist based on an interview and projective test responses indicated no major behavioral or emotional problems, although signs of increasing frustration in school were becoming evident.

The pediatrician then instituted medication for Alan since behavior modification programming alone had not been sufficient. Alan's previous behavioral program[11,12] was kept in place. Methylphenidate 5 mg in the morning and 5 mg at lunch time was added to the therapeutic approach. Improvement in Alan's school behavior was reflected by the teacher's ratings on the Conners Scale a few weeks later. Additional educational help was provided through special education resources soon thereafter.

In this example, the pediatrician's knowledge that learning problems often are found in hyperactive and attentionally deficient children allowed him to act as an advocate for the child educationally and to clarify further the nature of the child's problems in learning and behavior. Learning disabilities can significantly affect a child's behavior at home as well as in school. In this case, the child's problems with auditory processing would have served to stimulate the pediatrician to ask the parents a number of additional questions, such as whether the child seemed to "tune out," not pay attention, misunderstand, forget, or show a poor memory in the home environment. If the child was having problems in these areas, appropriate pediatric counseling about the nature of the problem and ways to deal with it (such as by repeating statements slowly, minimizing distractions when the auditory mode was used, and combining visual and auditory modalities), perhaps in consultation with the special education teacher, would have been in order.

CASE ILLUSTRATION 4

Chuck R. is a 6-year-old boy referred by his neurosurgeon to a pediatrician for ongoing general medical care. The history is one of relatively normal behavior and development until a few years ago. Chuck then became a somewhat anxious child who was afraid to try new tasks. He also appeared to have an inordinate fear of novel situations. He was a highly verbal child of seemingly average intelligence. Chuck's manner was to talk a great deal and to require numerous explanations from his parents and others. Marital discord was present and had culminated in separation and then in divorce in the few years preceding the current evaluation by the pediatrician. Further complicating matters had been the onset of headaches and other neurological symptoms about 18 months before. Chuck was ultimately evaluated by a neurosurgeon and found to have a brain tumor (a craniopharyngioma). This was treated surgically when Chuck was 4½ to 5 years old. The operative procedure and postoperative course went relatively smoothly, but soon thereafter, and especially on entering school, Chuck was noted to have an exacerbation of his anxiety and "obsessive" talking. He also began eating a great deal. Endocrinological and neurosurgical evidence indicated he had a decreased sense of satiety because of the tumor's destructive effects on the hypothalamus but that his excessive eating could be controlled behaviorally. In fact, advice about this had been given but not followed either by Chuck's mother or by his relatives, who felt understandably sorry for the child and unfortunately allowed him to eat as much as he wished and whenever he wished.

The result was that his weight was markedly over the 95th percentile for age, with his height at the 10th percentile for age. In school he performed adequately academically but did not play with other children, was extremely concerned about getting hurt or roughhousing with peers, asked endless questions and constantly needed verbal reassurance and a step-by-step description of whatever was going to happen next. Finally, in exasperation, the teacher suggested that he be checked by a doctor because of his "weight problem."

When interviewed by the pediatrician, the child was very verbal, quite bright, cooperative, and pleasant. He had a pseudo-adult explanation for everything and little ability to smile or to react emotionally. He spoke at great length in answer to questions, elaborated needlessly, maintained eye contact with the examiner and had a good sense of reality. He preferred to play board games when given a choice of playroom activities and preceded all movements and actions with verbal descriptions of what action he was going to take next or what action he had just completed. When asked to draw a picture of a person, he drew a figure that had weak stick like extensions for arms and legs and a large tongue protruding from the mouth, thus indicating his highly ineffectual self-concept with the need to compensate by excessive verbal and eating behaviors.

This child certainly needed ongoing pediatric care, and a pediatric referral was therefore arranged. A brief evaluation also indicated his considerable need for mental health involvement. The extent of the problems that he was experiencing (which involved reactions to a life-threatening disorder, brain surgery, and marital discord and divorce), as well as the severity and duration of the disturbance, made this child unsuitable for mental health involvement by a pediatric provider. Psychological testing was not needed to make this determination, although it might have provided information to the clinician working with the child and the mother about general pediatric issues and supportive care. The child was referred to a mental health center for further evaluation and treatment of his emotional problems.

In other situations the question of whether the child can be followed and treated for psychological problems by the primary health care provider is not so clear-cut as in this example.[13] Descriptors such as "of short duration," "not too severe," "reactive to a particular situation," "an exaggeration of a normal developmental occurrence," or "maintaining adequate functioning" may be used to justify following or treating the patient by the health care clinician without mental health consultation or referral. This approach can at times be detrimental to the child and family. Unfortunately there are presently no clear guidelines as to where the role of the primary health clinician leaves off and the role of the primary mental health care provider begins. The primary health care clinician's honest assessment of his or her own training, experience, and knowledge, along with a careful assessment of the child and family and possible use of behavior rating scales may make the decision about whether to begin treatment, continue treatment, or refer more likely to be correct. Additional help in making this decision may involve a one-time consultation with the child psychiatrist or child psychologist and/or the recommendation for psychological testing. The latter should provide an assessment of important emotional and behavioral issues in the child's life, as well as an assessment of intellectual and developmental functioning which, when abnormal, are often related to the child's emotional or behavioral problems. The results of psychological testing can also be used by the primary health care clinician to help justify or explain a recommendation to the parents and to the child for intensive treatment by a primary mental health clinician.

References

1. Gabel S: The primary health care provider's role in the provision of mental health services and the prevention of mental illness in children, in Gabel S (ed): *Behavioral Problems in Childhood: A Primary Care Approach*. New York, Grune & Stratton Inc., 1981.

2. Frankenburg WK, Dodds JB: The Denver Developmental Screening Test. *J Pediatr* 71:181, 1967.
3. Frankenburg WK, Randall AW, Sciarillo W, et al: The newly abbreviated and revised Denver Developmental Screening Test. *J Pediatr* 99:995, 1981.
4. Gabel S: Screening procedures, in Gabel S, Erickson MT (eds): *Child Development and Developmental Disabilities.* Boston, Little, Brown & Co, 1980.
5. Gabel S: Screening for developmental and behavioral problems in children, Gabel S (ed): *Behavioral Problems in Childhood: A Primary Care Approach.* New York, Grune & Stratton Inc, 1981.
6. Gabel S: The medical evaluation, in Gabel S, Erickson MT (eds): *Child Development and Developmental Disabilities.* Boston, Little, Brown & Co, 1980.
7. Gabel S: The general assessment, in Gabel S (ed): *Behavioral Problems in Childhood: A Primary Care Approach.* New York, Grune & Stratton Inc, 1981.
8. Conners CK: A teacher rating scale for use in drug studies with children. *Am J Psychiatry* 126:884, 1969.
9. Conners CK: Symptom patterns in hyperactive, neurotic and normal children. *Child Dev* 41:667, 1970.
10. Goyette CH, Conners CK, Ulrich RF: Normative data on revised Conners Parent and Teacher Rating Scales. *J Abnorm Child Psychol* 6:221, 1978.
11. Johnson SV: Behavioral management techniques, in Gabel S (ed): *Behavioral Problems in Childhood: A Primary Care Approach.* New York, Grune & Stratton Inc, 1981.
12. Safer DJ, Gabel S: The hyperactive behavioral pattern and associated symptoms, in Gabel S (ed): *Behavioral Problems in Childhood: A Primary Care Approach.* New York, Grune & Stratton Inc, 1981.
13. Johnson SB: Guidelines for short-term counseling, in Gabel S (ed): *Behavioral Problems in Childhood: A Primary Care Approach.* New York, Grune & Stratton Inc, 1981.

Chapter 3

The Referral for Psychological Testing

The previous chapter has given examples illustrating the types of children seen by pediatricians and other primary health care providers who may benefit from psychological testing. Children with developmental delays, children with various learning problems in the school environment, children who do not achieve academically to the degree expected by themselves or their parents, and children who have a variety of behavioral and emotional problems may all be referred for psychological testing by primary care physicians or other health and educational providers. This chapter will discuss the referral process for psychological testing and amplify further on the coordination and professional interaction between the physician and the psychologist.

Finding the Appropriate Psychologist

When the physician has decided to refer for psychological testing, he or she must first decide where to refer the child: to mental health agency, school, or private practitioner. The physician must also decide, if a referral is made to a private practitioner, which psychologist in the community would be best able to establish rapport with the child and provide capable assessment, whether that psychologist also includes in the testing session an interview with the parent(s) or not, and whether an interview with the parent(s) is necessary from the physician's perspective. Furthermore, how well the psychologist in question works with the physician in that subtle but crucial mix of personalities that either facilitates or impedes informal, productive communication must be taken into account. Also to be considered is the quality and adequacy of the psychological report ultimately produced by the psychologist. Will the report be helpful to the physician working with the child and family? Will it be helpful to other community agencies that may ultimately come to see it if appropriate parental permission is granted? Will the report be phrased in a manner that will be viewed as helpful and supportive (if at all possible) by parents should they ultimately have access to the report, as is often their legal right?

The physician also must know whether the psychologist to whom the referral is being made would be willing or able to take the child on as a therapy case if the physician requests this course subsequent to the psychological assessment or, as sometimes happens, whether the psychologist would be willing to act as a consultant to the health clinician if the latter requests this service as he or she continues to follow and treat the child and/or the family.

Finally, the health care clinician must consider (and should clarify) whether, and to what degree, the psychologist will discuss the test result with the parents and with the child after the testing session. Does the psychologist show flexibility on this point? Is the psychologist willing to explain the findings to parents or child if the physician feels uncomfortable with his or her knowledge in a particular area (e.g., the subtleties of perceptual difficulties in a child with a specific learning disability) or if the physician feels uncomfortable emotionally in informing parents of children with a particular type of problem (e.g., parents of a mentally retarded child)? Would the psychologist agree to a further session and a joint informing interview, with the physician explaining the medical aspects of the case (e.g., the medical tests to determine, if possible, the etiology of the child's mental retardation), while the psychologist discusses the testing process, procedures, and test data that contribute to the diagnosis of mental retardation?

Needless to say, the clinician's ability to control these variables involving the particular psychologist and his or her manner of handling the case is far greater if a referral is made to a private psychologist than when a referral is made to a mental health agency or to the school system. Some agencies, however, are more flexible and have sufficiently large staffs so that they do permit suggestions and do discuss who would be most appropriate to do the testing on the basis of the referral source's knowledge of the patient, the problem, and previous contacts with various psychologists in that school system or agency.

Even in the case of a private referral problems can arise, however. It is not always clear to the physician, especially if he or she is new to the community, exactly how to locate an appropriately trained and experienced psychologist for the testing referral and whether this course is in any case justifiable if finances are a consideration to the parents. In many cases insurance coverage may not be present or adequate, and the public schools may be the most obvious referral source since they have increasingly come to the fore as the public agency charged under recent laws (P.L. 94-142, and various state laws) with the assessment of children manifesting learning and behavior problems (at least in the school setting). Unfortunately, not all schools are equipped, funded, or able to perform a thorough evaluation on children even if the learning and behavior problems are at least partially present in the school environment. The quality of school and educational psychologists also varies considerably (as does the quality of other psychologists and physicians), and some school-affiliated psychologists emphasize mainly academic difficulties in their assessments or do not have the time to speak to parents to obtain a full psychosocial or developmental history that might add important background information about emotional and behavioral problems. Additionally, some parents wish to have obtained independent opinions from professionals outside the school system about their children's problems, especially since they are often asked, in part as a result of the testing, to consent to special class placement for their children.

If it is decided to choose a psychologist who works in private practice, and if the physician does not know an appropriately experienced and trained psychologist from past association, he or she can learn of potentially suitable psychologists by talking with physician colleagues who see children with learning and behavior problems (i.e., developmentally and behaviorally oriented pediatricians or child psychiatrists), by soliciting the help of prominent psychologists in the community (e.g., chairpersons of psychology departments at universities, heads of local professional groups), or by locating national or state psychological organizations (e.g., the American Psychological Association, 1200 Seventeenth Street, N.W., Washington, D.C. 20036) and inquiring about local affiliates who can make appropriate suggestions about psychologists working in the community.

This question of who is professionally appropriate to do psychological testing in children is important. There are considerable differences in qualifications and experience among psychologists. Designations preceding the term *psychologist* which are used by members of the profession and by licensing boards of various states reflect these differences. Terms such as *licensed, clinical, clinical child, educational*, and the like have particular meanings based, generally, on training or licensure requirements. These terms may, however, be confusing to the health care provider and hinder the latter's understanding of what services and expertise can be expected from a particular psychologist. When any question about the qualifications, experience, or licensure of the psychologist arises, it is best to clarify the question directly with the person concerned and possibly also with the licensing board in the area or with other practitioners in the area.

How Much Must the Physician Know about Psychological Tests?

The terms, concepts, assumptions, limitations, and benefits of psychological testing in children are rarely taught in any depth, if at all, in medical school or in postgraduate medical training. It is therefore understandable that primary care physicians often feel confused about psychological testing, uncertain about its uses and value, and ill at ease in making recommendations based on its findings. Several chapters in this book attempt to address a variety of these concerns and should permit a more rational basis for decisions concerning the use of psychological testing.

In the end, however, it is not possible to define the critical level of knowledge about psychological testing that is necessary for the health care provider. Certainly the more the clinician understands and feels at home with statistical concepts and terms (e.g., *reliability, validity, deviance, correlation*) that are so much a part of psychological test construction and description, the more intelligently the clinician can read psychological reports, communicate with psychologists, and explain findings to patients. The more thoroughly physicians understand assumptions, terms, and concepts involved in testing, the better able they will be to utilize psychological testing and reports to maximum benefit. The more physicians understand about the various tests, what different types of tests attempt to assess, and what individual tests within a particular group (e.g., Stanford-Binet versus WISC–R in the group of tests measuring cognitive functioning) share or do not share in terms of common assumptions or properties, the more effectively they will be able to use psychological testing. Yet different clinicians, based on their differing involvements in the psychological problems of children, will understandably pursue the area of testing to a greater or lesser degree.

It is not necessary for physicians, trained in medical approaches and not trained in psychological testing, to be overly anxious about their relative lack of expertise or depth of knowledge in this area. A counter weight to the physician's perceived lack of expertise may be his or her realization of this relative weakness and the assertive pursuit of understanding through reading, workshops, questioning, and active verbal communication with psychologists who do testing on the health care provider's patients. Psychologists who are able and willing to explain psychological test findings to the clinician verbally and in written reports using clear, concise terms and avoiding psychological jargon as much as possible should be sought. Psychologists who repeatedly fail to make themselves or their reports comprehensible to the health care clinician in practical terms that will ultimately allow the clinician to be most useful to the particular patient and family should not be consulted. Health care providers, in these cases, should search until they find a psychologist who appears to be both helpful and understandable. If a particular psychologist is too busy, difficult to talk with, or simply of a different temperament so that communication is difficult, it is appropriate to try and resolve differences but not appropriate, failing that, to continue consulting the same psychologist. Feeling ill at ease asking questions, having referral questions unanswered, having questions answered in incomprehensible terms, or feeling unable informally and honestly to discuss personal clinical weaknesses or areas of uncertainty about the patient's problems with the psychologist indicate that communication between the two professionals is not good and will ultimately result in detriment to the patient. This will be true regardless of whether the presumed fault lies with the psychologist or with the physician. Searching carefully for the most effective professional relationship of child health care provider and psychologist is well worth the effort and from the child health care provider's perspective can help compensate for the clinicians lack of expertise in the area of psychological testing.

Making the Referral

The psychologist engaged in the testing can be most helpful to the referring health care provider and to the provider's patients if the psychologist receives a clear, concise, direct statement verbally or in writing indicating what is known about the case, why the referral is being made, and what the referral source's expectations of the psychologist and of the testing are. What is the problem as understood by the patient and family (i.e., the chief complaint)? What is the problem at the current stage of the referring clinician's understanding based on his or her prior contacts with the family? What tests, procedures, or assessments have or have not already been done by the clinician (e.g., a developmental screening test may have been done, but a careful psychosocial history may not have been taken)? What procedures are contemplated based on, or regardless of, the psychological test results (e.g., computerized axial tomography scanning to elicit possible etiologies of mental retardation)? What are the roles and degrees of involvement as regards informing the parents and the child, ongoing therapy, and so on expected from the psychologist performing the testing, the referring clinician, or others subsequent to the psychological testing and other steps of the evaluation? What, if any, are significant additional areas of importance to the psychologist doing the testing (e.g., a history of severe mental illness in the family, a parent who has attempted suicide)?

It should be noted that nowhere in the foregoing list of referral questions and elaborations is mention made of the physician's or other child health provider's asking the psychologist to do a particular test or type of test. In making a referral to an appropriately trained and experienced psychologist, the clinician should assume that the psychologist's competence is greater than that of the health care provider in the area of psychological testing and that the psychologist is the most appropriate person to select one or more tests from the large number of tests available to address a particular question or problem. It is the professional competence of the psychologist who has had appropriate training and experience that renders him or her best able to make meaningful decisions about whether a standardized test of any type is appropriate in a given situation, which tests should be used, how to interpret the results, whether to add another test from a different group of tests to the test battery, and so on. These decisions involve far more than simply administering a test in a cookbook fashion and arriving at a score of one type or another. If the health care clinician lacks confidence in the psychologist's ability to make these judgments carefully and expertly, he should try to determine why he lacks this confidence, assess whether this lack of confidence is appropriate, and, if it is, find another psychologist with whom he can work more effectively. If the health care provider's lack of confidence appears inappropriate on further evaluation, the professional judgment of the psychologist in the area of psychological testing should be accepted. This approach is far preferable to trying to supervise, dictate, or arbitrarily question results obtained by another professional in a field that physicians and other health care providers should generally approach with an honest awareness of their own inexperience.

Chapter 4

The Psychological Report

The psychological report is the culmination of the referral process. Each section of the report attempts to provide the relevant data gathered during the testing session. The length, detail, and format of the psychological report vary depending on the purposes of the report, questions to be answered, complexity of the case, referral source, and, of course, the writing style of the psychologist. Ancillary information concerning the case is usually communicated either verbally or in writing by means of a cover letter to the referring clinician.

Several discrete areas of information are generally present in the formal psychological report. These include sections on:

1. Identifying information
2. Previous evaluations
3. Tests included in the present examination
4. Historical data and/or knowledge gained from interviewing the child and family
5. Behavioral observations
6. Test results and interpretations
7. Summary and impressions
8. Recommendations

This chapter attempts to elaborate upon each of these sections and then provides an example of a full report to familiarize the child health professional more fully with what to expect when he or she is in possession of a written evaluation.

The initial section of the report provides demographic information relating to the child, such as his or her name, age, birthdate, address, educational level, and name of school he or she is attending. Other information which is typically found in this section includes the date of testing, the name of the referral source, and a statement covering the questions asked in the referral. This latter statement is particularly salient since it is these questions that are to be answered in the report.

The next portion of the report mentions whether previous psychological testing has occurred. If this information is known, the names of the tests administered and a brief overview of the findings should be stated. With this knowledge, comparisons in functioning can be made.

The third section lists the various tests given during the current testing session and the results if the results can be presented numerically, as with IQ scores. Results of projective tests, such as the Rorschach or Figure Drawings, are usually not described in this manner. To some degree, the detailing of scores is a matter of preference and may reflect the anticipated usage of the report. In general, the more information given the better, at least from the viewpoint of the referring health care provider. For example, the referring physician might find it difficult to follow the psychologist's reasoning as to why a child is determined to have a specific learning disability on the basis of WISC-R findings unless specific scores and subtest "scatter" can be appreciated from the reported test results.

The fourth part provides a brief review of the history of the case as the psychologist understands it. This narrative may include information provided by the referring health care provider as well as information the psychologist has obtained by speaking with the parent(s) and/or with the child. The kinds of details that are normally included in this section include the family background and dynamics, specific antecedents and elaborations of referral questions (e.g., what were the precipitating events that led to a given child's being suspended from school), the parent's and/or child's perceptions of the problems, and the developmental and social history of the child.

A further portion of the report specifies the actual data gathered during the testing session and discusses the psychologist's observations of the child's behavior during the testing. Comments about the child's physical appearance, motivation, affect, activity level and interest in test materials, and problems of separation from the parent(s) might all be included. Here, the psychologist might mention how valid the test results seem and whether they reflect the best estimate of the child's actual current functioning. If the results do not seem valid, the psychologist should attempt to offer reasons for this conclusion (e.g., extreme anxiety about the testing environment, problems separating from the parents, excessive distractability) and suggest how these factors affected test performance and/or scores.

The next section provides detailed analysis and interpretation of the results of the various tests. In this discussion, an attempt is made to integrate the various test results concerning the child's intellect, academic knowledge, and emotional status into a coherent whole, showing how the child's strengths and shortcomings might impact on everyday situations to influence the child's growth and development. This section might also address the question of why a particular test was administered if this test was not a relatively standard part of the test battery for a child with that particular problem (e.g., choosing to administer the Leiter International Performance Scale to a hearing-impaired youngster with academic problems who would not be expected to perform to his or her maximal potential on the usual tests of intellectual abilities).

A narrative portion briefly summarizes the entire case and provides a short statement emphasizing essential findings and conclusions to be drawn from the test data and from observations made in spending time with the child. It offers a final impression of the psychologist's understanding of the child in relation to his or her problem areas. The psychologist tries to present well-reasoned hypotheses regarding the dynamics which are maintaining these problematic behaviors and also attempts to offer possible courses of action that the referring physician may want to explore further with the parents.

The last section provides a series (often a list) of specific recommendations concerning further diagnostic approaches or treatment strategies that the psychologist feels would be helpful to the child and family on the basis of his or her understanding of the child's needs. For instance, if psychotherapy is recommended, the psychologist should try to focus on the question of which type of treatment modality would be most effective. If further educational or neurological evaluations are deemed necessary from the test conclusions, then this should be explicitly stated. Again, this section should be as specific and comprehensive as possible.

Psychological Evaluation

Name: *Paul R.*
Date of birth: *July 23, 1970*
Date of testing: *January 18, 1983*
Age: *12 years, 6 months*

Education: 7th grade
School: W———— Junior High School
Referral source: Anna S., M.D., Children's Hospital and Clinic
Referral question: To assess present academic performance and
   recommend appropriate interventions as necessay.

Present Evaluation

Wechsler Intelligence Scale for Children—Revised (WISC–R)
Wide Range Achievement Test (WRAT)
Bender Visual-Motor Gestalt Test
Family Drawing
Thematic Apperception Test (TAT)

BACKGROUND INFORMATION AND FAMILY INTERVIEW

Paul R. is a 12-year-old boy, the youngest and only son of
four children born to Michael and Joyce R. The father, age 46, is
presently a supervisor at a trucking company, where he has been
employed for approximately 17 years. The mother, age 49, currently
teaches fifth grade at the same school (W———— Junior High School)
where Paul is enrolled. In fact, Mrs. R. was Paul's teacher when he
was in fifth grade. She has been a teacher in both public and private
schools for 28 years. Paul's two oldest sisters (Jo Ellen, age 21, and
Maggie, age 19) are both attending college on academic scholar-
ships. According to the mother, the oldest (Jo Ellen) is the brightest
of the three girls, and Maggie is the most attractive, having previously been chosen as a homecoming queen. Nancy, age 17, is
still at home and is a senior in high school. Reportedly, she experienced academic problems in both elementary school and high
school, and she is considered quite "independent with a strong
personality."

This referral was precipitated by a recent teacher's conference
regarding Paul's present functioning and adjustment to the seventh
grade. Paul's teacher told Mr. R. (because of her position, Mrs. R
does not attend these meetings) that Paul apparently had been
inattentive in class, had not been completing his assignments, and
had been observed humming to himself on many occasions during
class. According to the mother, this is the first year that Paul has
experienced academic difficulties; previously he had been viewed
as a solid "B" student. Reportedly, his most readily observable
academic weakness at this time is mathematics, but official
school reports were not available when this evaluation was
written.

Developmentally, Paul apparently has experienced some

physical difficulties. According to the mother, he had food allergies from age 5 months to approximately 2½ years. He also had respiratory problems prior to age 2, causing two hospitalizations. He was, in fact, susceptible to many colds until age 10. Paul was also described as being afraid of the dark and as being an early riser. He used to sleep with a vaporizer and apparently still requires a humming sound to fall asleep. Mrs. R. felt that these early complications made her react in a protective manner toward Paul. Additionally, she recalled that Paul's toilet training had occurred later than that of his siblings (at approximately 3 years of age) and that he was a bedwetter until age 4. Paul's milestones concerning walking and talking were well within the normal range and even slightly advanced, according to his mother.

The parents' perspectives on the presenting problem seemed to differ markedly. The father perceived Paul as having problems similar to some which he had experienced when he was Paul's age. He revealed that he had been raised in a different atmosphere and that education had not been emphasized. He recalled not having had to work very hard in school and, because of "natural" abilities, was able to "get away with a lot." He did not view Paul as having the academic skills required to perform at a higher level without providing maximum effort. The mother possesses a strong regard for education and has attempted to instill this value in all family members. She apparently also possesses strong religious convictions and, despite the father's Lutheran orientation, has raised the family in the Roman Catholic tradition. When queried as to what might have occurred during the past year to exacerbate Paul's problems, the mother said that her father (age 79) had suffered a stroke and had subsequently moved into their household. She believes that caring for her ailing father has required her to redirect much of the attention which she formerly focused on Paul.

Paul was unable to elaborate upon his present problems. His main focus concerned the difficulty in his academic work, which he reports is becoming harder for him to complete. He also indicated that he is having peer problems and does not enjoy the company of his classmates. He did mention, though, that he has neighborhood friends, especially one male youth to whom he is particularly close. Additionally, Paul said that he had run for student council office and had tried out for the basketball and track teams. However, all these attempts met with failure. He discussed an interest in playing football, but the mother has discouraged this sport in the past. Currently, his only extracurricular school activity is singing in the choir. At home, Paul has assigned chores within the household and privileges which are revoked as punishment. He also works in the neighborhood, doing such tasks as taking care of animals and shoveling snow, to earn money.

Behavioral Observations

Paul presented as a heavyset, socially awkward child who was well-mannered, compliant, and soft-spoken. He was clad in a sweatshirt and jeans for the evaluation. He was righthanded and held a pencil in an artistic manner (two fingers and thumb extended) which caused him to write or draw in a sketchy style. His affect was initially very constricted, but this early sign of anxiety appeared to subside after a while. He seemed to be challenged by all of the presented tasks, but was distractible during any delay in presentation. It was as though he became quickly bored when the external structure of the situation was removed. His style during the tasks was very plodding and ruminative, causing him to lose some points on speeded tasks. He was particularly attentive to detail; however, on certain problems (especially math) he would overlook things (e.g., decimal point placement), which lowered his scores. On some tasks, he made self-critical statements, and initially he needed encouraging statements before continuing. This was particularly evident in his drawings, when he stated, "I can't draw people" and erased constantly. Overall, his test-taking behavior seemed sporadic but probably reflected accurately his present level of functioning.

Test Results and Interpretations

On the administration of the WISC–R, Paul obtained a Verbal Scale IQ score of 120, a Performance Scale IQ score of 120, with a resulting Full Scale IQ score of 123. This latter score places him within the superior range of intellectual functioning and appears to be valid. Although little disparity existed between the Verbal and Performance scores, there was considerable variation among the subtests. The following list of obtained scores represents this scattering:

Information	12	Picture Completion	15
Similarities	15	Picture Arrangement	11
Arithmetic	10	Block Design	14
Vocabulary	12	Object Assembly	15
Comprehension	18	Coding	9
Digit Span	10		

These subtest scores indicate that Paul has several particularly outstanding abilities. Most notable among these is his knowledge of societal norms and expectations. This portion of the WISC-R (i.e., Comprehension) is designed to gauge judgment and common sense. Success is dependent on the possession of practical information and the ability to evaluate and utilize previous experience. Other areas of strength for Paul include such skills as verbal concept formation (abstract thinking), logical thinking, visual alertness, concentration, and perceptual organization. His less well developed abilities, although still within the average range, include mental arithmetic reasoning, short-term memory, and psychomotor speed. Because success on these tasks (Arithmetic, Digit Span, Coding) would require attention and concentration, this finding provides support for the possibility that an attentional deficit or a specific learning disability in the visual or auditory processing area might be affecting Paul's performance.

On the WRAT, Paul attained grade level scores of 7.0, 5.3, and 7.9 on the Spelling, Arithmetic, and Reading portions, respectively. Thus, he appears to be behind his current grade placement in Spelling by approximately one-half of a grade level and in Arithmetic by approximately 2¼ years. His ability to pronounce words seems to reflect his current grade standing. These average to below-average findings are quite remarkable considering Paul's demonstrated intellectual abilities on the WISC-R.

Results from Paul's Bender did not provide evidence of any perceptual-motor dysfunction or implicate any organic factors as possible contributants to his scholastic problems. There were no scorable errors, indicating that Paul has reached a perceptual maturational level commensurate with his age. However, there was some suggestion of emotional difficulties within the protocol. It seems as though Paul has strong attentional needs, is somewhat emotionally labile, and possesses poor planning ability. When the Bender designs were removed from view, Paul was able to reproduce eight of the nine figures, demonstrating exceptional ability in short-term memory.

An attempt to get Paul to complete a family drawing was terminated because Paul took too long a time to complete the project. Again, the partial drawing demonstrated his need to be the center of attention. Also, it showed an excessively controlled, anxious style of performing. This was particularly evident in the amount of detail within the picture and the sketchiness of the figures. The family drawing showed three distinct groupings of family members. Paul seemed to indicate a closeness among himself, his father, and his sister who still lives at home; the two older sisters formed another cluster. The mother appeared as isolated from the family members but as director of household activities.

Results from the TAT indicated that Paul tended to feel insecure and to possess a great need for attention. He seemed to be easily influenced by others and overly responsive to others' evaluations rather than to his own. He appeared likely to react to frustration by punishing himself or by exhibiting sad moods. He also tended to be narcissistic and demanding of sympathy. Additional themes of sadness, frustration, and hostility were also portrayed. It appeared that Paul becomes easily upset and is prone to act out his feelings. There were also conflictual themes regarding parental love and striving for acceptance. This latter problem might well respond to psychotherapeutic intervention.

Summary and Impressions

Paul presents as a bright, well-behaved pubescent youth who appears to be experiencing adjustment reactions to both academic and social demands. He is somewhat overweight, motorically awkward, and appears timid and hesitant in social situations. Intellectual testing suggests that he possesses considerable positive attributes and potential; yet he is moderately delayed in certain areas of basic academic skills, especially arithmetic computation. These academic problems may be attributable to either attentional deficits or a specific learning disability. Paul also appears to be emotionally constricted, overly sensitive to criticism and possible rejection, and conflicted by attentional and dependency needs. Combined, these problems may be impeding his maturational development and are probably contributing to a fragile self-image.

Paul seems to have developed a ruminative, reflective style of problem solving that represents only a marginally effective mechanism for reducing anxiety. This style probably appears to others as procrastination and indecisiveness, which may create many frustrating interpersonal exchanges with those individuals who expect Paul to produce quicker responses to their questions. In turn, this negative feedback may be creating an emotional distance between Paul and others. This seems to be reflected in his lack of involvement with school peers.

Paul also appears to have internalized many regulations from society and his family, and this seems to have created many restrictions on his actions. He apparently has overlearned what is proper behavior and has instilled this in his personal repertoire. However, this too seems to be creating a gap between him and more spontaneous peers. In his struggle to control his behavior, he has adopted many immature ways of expressing possible feelings of anger. It is noteworthy that the presenting problem is academic—an area of significant importance to the mother. It is also interesting that Paul was protected as a child (being the only male), and it is likely that this is related to some of the emotional problems which are now surfacing.

It is important that a remediative avenue be explored with the parents to circumvent the self-defeating cycle which has enveloped Paul. The family should be encouraged to accept a recommendation of counseling for the family in order to enhance self-exploration and aid in the understanding of how Paul's emotional problems may influence his performance. Since the referral was approached from an academic standpoint, it might be that the parents will want to concentrate within that sphere only. However, it would be highly beneficial for the family to engage in counseling in order to understand better the breadth of psychological factors which appear to contribute to the maintenance of Paul's probable academic and social behavior.

Recommendations

1. At this time, Paul could benefit significantly from a relationship with a supportive individual. Therefore, individual or peer group therapy would be deemed appropriate, with emphasis on social skills training, acceptance of adolescent change, and increased spontaneity, which, it is believed, would produce a freer expression of affect.

2. Consideration should also be given to therapeutic sessions with Paul's parents and/or the entire family, to provide a broader network for resolving family conflicts. The family appears to have many mixed values which are probably confusing to Paul and need clarifying. Also, the parents seem currently to be ignoring Paul's intellectual talents (possibly because of comparisons with his older sisters or his current academic problems). This perception seems to be impeding Paul's development and should be explored during counseling.

3. It would be helpful for Paul if the parents could arrange for academic remediation on a one-to-one tutorial basis. He remains behind in all areas of scholastic aptitude, especially arithmetic, despite intellectual ability considered to be superior. Providing individual instruction would also help in overcoming Paul's attentional problems.

4. A more thorough educational evaluation should be performed to clarify specific academic weaknesses and/or disabilities. Recommendations based on this examination could benefit the school and the tutor in developing an individualized treatment plan.

Chapter 5

Behavior Rating Scales

Behavior Rating Scales

Behavior rating scales provide objective information about the observable behavior problems of preschool children, school-aged children, and teenagers. Typically completed by a child's parent and/or teacher, these rating scales can be used for a number of purposes including clarifying whether or not a particular child has a significant behavior problem, targeting specific behaviors that require direct intervention, and assessing the impact of an intervention strategy.

Many rating scales are empirically based with their structures or categories based on the results of factor analysis. In this statistical procedure, raters' scores on a number of observable behaviors are intercorrelated in a way that permits behaviors to be identified as clustering together. Most empirical studies of children's behavior problems produce two major clusters: one set of behaviors is reflective of "internalized" symptoms such as phobias, somatic complaints, withdrawal, and crying, and another set of behaviors is reflective of externalized symptoms including disobedience, stealing, lying, and fighting.[1] It is of note that these two-symptom clusters have emerged in numerous studies employing a number of different rating scales and focusing on a number of different populations of children.[2] Studies vary, however, in identifying more specific and refined clusters of behaviors. For example, some scales produce a "hyperactive" cluster and others do not.[2]

Various cautions have to be considered when using a behavior rating scale.[3] Most frequently cited is the lack of agreement that can occur between raters rating the same child. Interrater agreement is typically higher in scales that make use of behaviors that are operationally defined with little need for the rater to make inferences or interpretations. For example, "cries easily" is more readily observable than "appears depressed" and likely will produce higher agreement between raters.

Many studies report lower interrater agreement between parents and teachers than between parents.[3] Because school and home present different situational demands on a child, this low agreement is not surprising. Some rating scales now include different checklists for parents and teachers in order to account for the different situations the child faces in these two environments.[4]

Three of the most frequently used checklists are discussed in the following sections. A case illustration accompanies the Child Behavior Checklist Section.

Conners' Teacher Rating Scale and Conners' Parent's Questionnaire

Conners has developed separate scales for parents and teachers for the purpose of identifying behavior problems in school-aged children. The Conners' Parent's Questionnaire[5] consists of 93 items assessing a number of behavior problems including hyperactivity, fears and worries, sex problems, perfectionism, and bowel problems. The parent rates each item on a four-point Degree of Activity scale with "not at all" = 0, "just a little" = 1, "pretty much" = 2, and "very much" = 3. Factor analysis of the items has revealed six factors that Conners labeled aggressive conduct disorder, anxious-inhibited, antisocial, enuresis–encopresis, psychosomatic, and anxious–immature.

The Conners' Teacher Rating Scale[6] consists of 39 items presented in three clusters: classroom behavior, group participation, and attitude toward authority. The teacher rates each item on the same four-point scale described for the parent's questionnaire. Four behavioral clusters have emerged from factor analysis[7]: conduct problem, inattentive–passive, tension–anxiety, and hyperactivity. Research efforts have provided normative data[7] and have confirmed the usefulness of the scale in assessing hyperactivity in the classroom.[8,9]

Conners also developed an abbreviated teacher rating scale using the 10 items from the original 39 most often checked by teachers.[6] These 10 items have been shown to be reliable both in identifying hyperactive children and in assessing response to medication.[7] Satisfactory correlations have been found between the abbreviated teacher scale and the complete teacher scale.[7]

Like the other Conners rating scales, these 10 items are rated on a four-point degree of activity basis with 0 for "not at all" and 3 for "very much." A total score of 15 classifies a child as hyperactive on this abbreviated scale.

The ten items include: (1) restless or overactive; (2) excitable, impulsive; (3) disturbs other children; (4) fails to finish things he starts, short attention span; (5) constantly fidgeting; (6) inattentive, easily distracted; (7) demands must be met immediately, easily frustrated; (8) cries often and easily; (9) mood changes quickly and drastically; and (10) temper outbursts, explosive and unpredictable behavior.

Despite the Conners scales' popularity among pediatricians and mental health professionals, criticism has accumulated regarding some of the items and rating choices.[10] Several items are thought to lack clear behavioral descriptions (e.g., "submissive") which may lead to the rater's relying on generalizations about the child rather than considering specific behaviors. Other items may be difficult to rate because they contain more than one behavior (e.g., "demands must be met immediately, short attention span"). The rating choices have been criticized as being poorly defined with different raters making different assumptions about what "just a little" or "pretty much" means. Many of these problems can be overcome by providing brief training for raters to alert them to possible sources of rating error.

Conners has developed the *Revised Parent and Teacher Rating Scales*,[11] but they are not as thorough or reliable as the originals. The revisions were intended to simplify administration and interpretation. A 10-item Hyperkinesis Index can be calculated from each form.

Child Behavior Checklist

The Child Behavior Checklist and Revised Child Behavior Profile[4] represent the culmination of several years of research by Achenbach. The scale itself consists of two parts: one for assessing the child's social competencies and one for assessing behavior problems (see Figures 1a, b and 2a, b). The social competence scale consists of 20 items addressing out-of-school activities, social relations, and overall academic functioning. Behavior problems are assessed with a 113-item checklist with each item rated by the child's parent on a three-point basis for frequency

CHILD BEHAVIOR CHECKLIST FOR AGES 4-16

CHILD'S NAME

PARENT'S TYPE OF WORK *(Please be specific—for example: auto mechanic, high school teacher, homemaker, laborer, lathe operator, shoe salesman, army sergeant, even if parent does not live with child.)*

SEX ☐ Boy ☐ Girl   AGE   RACE

FATHER'S TYPE OF WORK:_____

TODAY'S DATE   CHILD'S BIRTHDATE

MOTHER'S TYPE OF WORK:_____

Mo. _____ Day _____ Yr. _____   Mo. _____ Day _____ Yr. _____

THIS FORM FILLED OUT BY:

☐ Mother

GRADE IN SCHOOL

☐ Father

☐ Other *(Specify):*

I. Please list the sports your child most likes to take part in. For example: swimming, baseball, skating, skate boarding, bike riding, fishing, etc.

☐ None

	Compared to other children of the same age, about how much time does he/she spend in each?				Compared to other children of the same age, how well does he/she do each one?			
	Don't Know	Less Than Average	Average	More Than Average	Don't Know	Below Average	Average	Above Average
a. _____	☐	☐	☐	☐	☐	☐	☐	☐
b. _____	☐	☐	☐	☐	☐	☐	☐	☐
c. _____	☐	☐	☐	☐	☐	☐	☐	☐

II. Please list your child's favorite hobbies, activities, and games, other than sports. For example: stamps, dolls, books, piano, crafts, singing, etc. (Do not include T.V.)

☐ None

	Compared to other children of the same age, about how much time does he/she spend in each?				Compared to other children of the same age, how well does he/she do each one?			
	Don't Know	Less Than Average	Average	More Than Average	Don't Know	Below Average	Average	Above Average
a. _____	☐	☐	☐	☐	☐	☐	☐	☐
b. _____	☐	☐	☐	☐	☐	☐	☐	☐
c. _____	☐	☐	☐	☐	☐	☐	☐	☐

III. Please list any organizations, clubs, teams, or groups your child belongs to.

☐ None

	Compared to other children of the same age, how active is he/she in each?			
	Don't Know	Less Active	Average	More Active
a. _____	☐	☐	☐	☐
b. _____	☐	☐	☐	☐
c. _____	☐	☐	☐	☐

IV. Please list any jobs or chores your child has. For example: paper route, babysitting, making bed, etc.

☐ None

	Compared to other children of the same age, how well does he/she carry them out?			
	Don't Know	Below Average	Average	Above Average
a. _____	☐	☐	☐	☐
b. _____	☐	☐	☐	☐
c. _____	☐	☐	☐	☐

3-81 Edition

Figure 1a. The social competence checklist from the Child Behavior Checklist. (Checklist copyright 1981 by Thomas M. Achenbach and used by permission.)

V. 1. About how many close friends does your child have? ☐ None ☐ 1 ☐ 2 or 3 ☐ 4 or more

2. About how many times a week does your child do things with them? ☐ less than 1 ☐ 1 or 2 ☐ 3 or more

VI. Compared to other children of his/her age, how well does your child:

		Worse	About the same	Better
a.	Get along with his/her brothers & sisters?	☐	☐	☐
b.	Get along with other children?	☐	☐	☐
c.	Behave with his/her parents?	☐	☐	☐
d.	Play and work by himself/herself?	☐	☐	☐

VII. 1. Current school performance—for children aged 6 and older:

☐ Does not go to school

	Failing	Below average	Average	Above average
a. Reading or English	☐	☐	☐	☐
b. Writing	☐	☐	☐	☐
c. Arithmetic or Math	☐	☐	☐	☐
d. Spelling	☐	☐	☐	☐
Other academic subjects—for example: history, science, foreign language, geography. e. _____	☐	☐	☐	☐
f. _____	☐	☐	☐	☐
g. _____	☐	☐	☐	☐

2. Is your child in a special class?

☐ No ☐ Yes—what kind?

3. Has your child ever repeated a grade?

☐ No ☐ Yes—grade and reason

4. Has your child had any academic or other problems in school?

☐ No ☐ Yes—please describe

When did these problems start?

Have these problems ended?

☐ No ☐ Yes—when?

Below is a list of items that describe children. For each item that describes your child **now or within the past 6 months**, please circle the 2 if the item is **very true or often true** of your child. Circle the 1 if the item is **somewhat or sometimes true** of your child. If the item is **not true** of your child, circle the 0. Please answer all items as well as you can, even if some do not seem to apply to your child.

0 = Not True (as far as you know) 1 = Somewhat or Sometimes True 2 = Very True or Often True

0 1 2	1.	Acts too young for his/her age	16	0 1 2	31.	Fears he/she might think or do something bad	
0 1 2	2.	Allergy (describe): _____					
				0 1 2	32.	Feels he/she has to be perfect	
				0 1 2	33.	Feels or complains that no one loves him/her	
0 1 2	3.	Argues a lot					
0 1 2	4.	Asthma		0 1 2	34.	Feels others are out to get him/her	
				0 1 2	35.	Feels worthless or inferior	50
0 1 2	5.	Behaves like opposite sex	20				
0 1 2	6.	Bowel movements outside toilet		0 1 2	36.	Gets hurt a lot, accident-prone	
				0 1 2	37.	Gets in many fights	
0 1 2	7.	Bragging, boasting					
0 1 2	8.	Can't concentrate, can't pay attention for long		0 1 2	38.	Gets teased a lot	
				0 1 2	39.	Hangs around with children who get in trouble	
0 1 2	9.	Can't get his/her mind off certain thoughts; obsessions (describe): _____		0 1 2	40.	Hears things that aren't there (describe): _____	
0 1 2	10.	Can't sit still, restless, or hyperactive	25				55
				0 1 2	41.	Impulsive or acts without thinking	
0 1 2	11.	Clings to adults or too dependent					
0 1 2	12.	Complains of loneliness		0 1 2	42.	Likes to be alone	
				0 1 2	43.	Lying or cheating	
0 1 2	13.	Confused or seems to be in a fog					
0 1 2	14	Cries a lot		0 1 2	44.	Bites fingernails	
				0 1 2	45.	Nervous, highstrung, or tense	60
0 1 2	15.	Cruel to animals	30				
0 1 2	16.	Cruelty, bullying, or meanness to others		0 1 2	46.	Nervous movements or twitching (describe): _____	
0 1 2	17.	Day-dreams or gets lost in his/her thoughts					
0 1 2	18.	Deliberately harms self or attempts suicide		0 1 2	47.	Nightmares	
0 1 2	19.	Demands a lot of attention		0 1 2	48.	Not liked by other children	
0 1 2	20.	Destroys his/her own things	35	0 1 2	49.	Constipated, doesn't move bowels	
0 1 2	21.	Destroys things belonging to his/her family or other children		0 1 2	50.	Too fearful or anxious	65
0 1 2	22.	Disobedient at home		0 1 2	51.	Feels dizzy	
				0 1 2	52.	Feels too guilty	
0 1 2	23.	Disobedient at school		0 1 2	53.	Overeating	
0 1 2	24.	Doesn't eat well					
				0 1 2	54.	Overtired	
0 1 2	25.	Doesn't get along with other children	40	0 1 2	55.	Overweight	70
0 1 2	26.	Doesn't seem to feel guilty after misbehaving			56.	Physical problems without known medical cause:	
0 1 2	27.	Easily jealous		0 1 2	a.	Aches or pains	
0 1 2	28.	Eats or drinks things that are not food (describe): _____		0 1 2	b.	Headaches	
				0 1 2	c.	Nausea, feels sick	
				0 1 2	d.	Problems with eyes (describe):	
0 1 2	29.	Fears certain animals, situations, or places, other than school (describe): _____		0 1 2	e.	Rashes or other skin problems	75
				0 1 2	f.	Stomachaches or cramps	
				0 1 2	g.	Vomiting, throwing up	
0 1 2	30.	Fears going to school	45	0 1 2	h.	Other (describe): _____	

Please see other side

Figure 1b. The behavior problems checklist from the Child Behavior Checklist. (Checklist copyright 1981 by Thomas M. Achenbach and used by permission.)

0 1 2	57.	Physically attacks people		0 1 2	84.	Strange behavior (describe): _____
0 1 2	58.	Picks nose, skin, or other parts of body (describe): _____				
		_____ 80		0 1 2	85.	Strange ideas (describe):
0 1 2	59.	Plays with own sex parts in public 16				
0 1 2	60.	Plays with own sex parts too much		0 1 2	86.	Stubborn, sullen, or irritable
0 1 2	61.	Poor school work		0 1 2	87.	Sudden changes in mood or feelings
0 1 2	62.	Poorly coordinated or clumsy		0 1 2	88.	Sulks a lot 45
0 1 2	63.	Prefers playing with older children 20		0 1 2	89.	Suspicious
0 1 2	64.	Prefers playing with younger children		0 1 2	90.	Swearing or obscene language
0 1 2	65.	Refuses to talk		0 1 2	91.	Talks about killing self
0 1 2	66.	Repeats certain acts over and over; compulsions (describe): _____		0 1 2	92.	Talks or walks in sleep (describe):
				0 1 2	93.	Talks too much 50
0 1 2	67.	Runs away from home		0 1 2	94.	Teases a lot
0 1 2	68.	Screams a lot 25				
				0 1 2	95.	Temper tantrums or hot temper
0 1 2	69.	Secretive, keeps things to self		0 1 2	96.	Thinks about sex too much
0 1 2	70.	Sees things that aren't there (describe):				
				0 1 2	97.	Threatens people
				0 1 2	98.	Thumb-sucking 55
		_____		0 1 2	99.	Too concerned with neatness or cleanliness
				0 1 2	100.	Trouble sleeping (describe):
0 1 2	71.	Self-conscious or easily embarrassed				
0 1 2	72.	Sets fires				_____
0 1 2	73.	Sexual problems (describe):		0 1 2	101.	Truancy, skips school
				0 1 2	102.	Underactive, slow moving, or lacks energy
				0 1 2	103.	Unhappy, sad, or depressed 60
		_____ 30		0 1 2	104.	Unusually loud
0 1 2	74.	Showing off or clowning				
0 1 2	75.	Shy or timid		0 1 2	105.	Uses alcohol or drugs (describe):
0 1 2	76.	Sleeps less than most children				_____
0 1 2	77.	Sleeps more than most children during day and/or night (describe): _____		0 1 2	106.	Vandalism
				0 1 2	107.	Wets self during the day
				0 1 2	108.	Wets the bed 65
0 1 2	78.	Smears or plays with bowel movements 35		0 1 2	109.	Whining
				0 1 2	110.	Wishes to be of opposite sex
0 1 2	79.	Speech problem (describe): _____		0 1 2	111.	Withdrawn, doesn't get involved with others
				0 1 2	112.	Worrying
0 1 2	80.	Stares blankly			113.	Please write in any problems your child has that were not listed above:
0 1 2	81.	Steals at home				
0 1 2	82.	Steals outside the home		0 1 2		_____ 70
0 1 2	83.	Stores up things he/she doesn't need (describe): _____ 40		0 1 2		_____
				0 1 2		_____

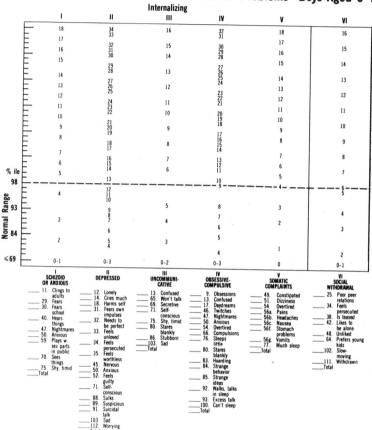

Figure 2a. Profile used for boys 6–11 to assess behavior problems on the Revised Child Behavior Profile. (Profile copyright 1982 by Thomas M. Achenbach and used by permission.)

(0 = "not at all," 1 = "occasionally," 2 = "frequently, often"). The entire scale requires about 17 minutes to complete.

Extensive normative work has produced two "broad band" factors (Internalizing and Externalizing) and nine "narrow band" factors. Five of the narrow band scales are subsumed under the Internalizing Scale: Schizoid, Depressed, Uncommunicative, Obsessive–Compulsive, and Somatic Complaints. Three of the other four narrow band scales fall within the Externalizing Scale: Hyperactive, Aggressive, and Delinquent. Social Withdrawal emerges as a separate factor for some age and

Externalizing

VII	VIII	IX	T Score
22	46 45 44 43	24	100
21		23 22	
20	42 41	21 20	95
19	40 39 38	19 18	
18	37	17	90
17	36 35 34	16 15	
16	33 32	14 13	85
15	31 30	12	
14	29 28 27 26	11 10	80
13	25 24	9 8	
12	23	7	75
11	22 21 20	6	
	19		70
10 9 8 7	17-18	5 4	
6	16	3	65
	15		
	13-14	2	60
5	12 11	1	
4 0-3	10 0-9	0	55

VII HYPERACTIVE

___ 1. Acts too young
___ 8. Can't concentrate
___ 10. Hyperactive
___ 13. Confused
___ 17. Daydreams
___ 20. Destroys own things
___ 41. Impulsive
___ 61. Poor schoolwork
___ 62. Clumsy
___ 64. Prefers young kids
___ 79. Speech problem
___ Total

VIII AGGRESSIVE

___ 3. Argues
___ 7. Brags
___ 16. Cruel to others
___ 19. Demands attention
___ 22. Disobeys at home
___ 23. Disobeys at school
___ 25. Poor peer relations
___ 27. Jealous
___ 37. Fights
___ 43. Lies, cheats
___ 48. Unliked
___ 57. Attacks people
___ 68. Screams
___ 74. Shows off
___ 86. Stubborn
___ 87. Moody
___ 88. Sulks
___ 90. Swearing
___ 93. Excess talk
___ 94. Teases
___ 95. Temper
___ 97. Threatens
___ 104. Loud
___ Total

IX DELINQUENT

___ 20. Destroys own things
___ 21. Destroys others' things
___ 23. Disobeys at school
___ 39. Bad friends
___ 67. Runs away
___ 72. Sets fires
___ 81. Steals at home
___ 82. Steals outside home
___ 90. Swearing
___ 101. Truant
___ 106. Vandalism
___ Total

Name _____

Case # _____
Filled out by _____
Age _____
Date _____
Sum Int _____
Int $\underline{T}$ _____
Sum Ext _____
Ext $\underline{T}$ _____
No. of items _____
Sum _____
Sum $\underline{T}$ _____

OTHER PROBLEMS

___ 2. Allergy
___ 4. Asthma
___ 5. Acts like opposite sex
___ 6. Encopresis
___ 15. Cruel to animals
___ 24. Doesn't eat well
___ 26. Lacks guilt
___ 28. Eats nonfood
___ 36. Accident prone
___ 44. Nailbiting
___ 53. Overeats
___ 55. Overweight
___ 56d. Eye problems
___ 56e. Rashes
___ 56h. Other phys. problems
___ 58. Picking
___ 60. Plays w. sex parts too much
___ 63. Prefers older kids
___ 73. Sex probs.
___ 78. Smears b.m.
___ 96. Sex preocc.
___ 98. Thumbsucking
___ 99. Too neat
___ 105. Alcohol, drug
___ 107. Wets self
___ 108. Wets bed
___ 109. Whining
___ 110. Wish to be opposite sex
___ 113. Other problems
___ Total

Internalizing			Externalizing		
Item	Total	T	Item	Total	T
___ 9.	0	35	___ 1.	0	31
___ 11.	1	39	___ 3.	1	37
___ 12.	2	41	___ 7.	2	40
___ 13.	3	43	___ 8.	3	41
___ 14.	4	46	___ 10.	4	43
___ 17.	5	48	___ 13.	5	44
___ 18.	6	49	___ 16.	6	46
___ 29.	7	51	___ 17.	7	48
___ 30.	8	52	___ 19.	8	49
___ 31.	9	54	___ 20.	9	51
___ 32	10	56	___ 21.	10	52
___ 33.	11	57	___ 22.	11	53
___ 34.	12	58	___ 23.	12-13	55
___ 35.	13	59	___ 25.	14	56
___ 40.	14	60	___ 27.	15	57
___ 45.	15	61	___ 37.	16	58
___ 46.	16	63	___ 39.	17	59
___ 47.	17-18	64	___ 41.	18	60
___ 49.	19	65	___ 43.	19	61
___ 50.	20	66	___ 48.	20-21	62
___ 51.	21-23	67	___ 57.	22	63
___ 52.	24-25	68	___ 61.	23-24	65
___ 54.	26-27	69	___ 62.	25	66
___ 56a.	28	70	___ 64.	26-27	67
___ 56b.	29-30	71	___ 67.	28	68
___ 56c.	31-32	72	___ 68.	29	69
___ 56f.	33-34	73	___ 72.	30-31	70
___ 56g.	35-36	74	___ 74.	32-33	71
___ 59.	37-38	75	___ 79.	34-35	72
___ 65.	39-40	76	___ 81.	36-37	73
___ 66.	41-42	77	___ 82.	38-39	74
___ 69.	43-44	78	___ 86.	40-41	75
___ 70.	45-46	79	___ 87.	42-44	76
___ 71.	47-48	80	___ 88.	45-46	77
___ 75.	49-50	81	___ 90.	47-48	78
___ 76.	51-52	82	___ 93.	49-50	79
___ 77.	53-54	83	___ 94.	51-52	80
___ 80.	55-56	84	___ 95.	53-54	81
___ 83.	57-58	85	___ 97.	55-56	82
___ 84.	59-60	86	___ 101.	57-59	83
___ 85.	61-62	87	___ 104.	60-61	84
___ 86.	63-64	88	___ 106.	62-63	85
___ 88.	65-67	89	___ Total	64-65	86
___ 89.	68-70	90		66-67	87
___ 91.	71-73	91		68-69	88
___ 92.	74-76	92		70-71	89
___ 93.	77-79	93		72	90
___ 100.	80-83	94		73	91
___ 103.	84-86	95		74-75	92
___ 112.	87-89	96		76	93
___ Total	90-92	97		77	94
	93-95	98		78	95
	96-98	99		79	96
	99-100	100		80-81	97
				82	98
				83	99
				84	100

sex groups. Achenbach provides separate norm profiles for boys and girls and for three age groupings: 4–5, 6–11, and 12–16 years. It should be noted that although the Internalizing–Externalizing factors exist in all six profiles the original factor analytic work did not produce the same narrow band factors for all of the sex and age groups. For example, hyperactivity did not appear as a factor for boys 4–5 years old.

Standard scores with a mean of 50 and a standard deviation of 10 are calculated for the two broad band factors and for the narrow band

REVISED CHILD BEHAVIOR PROFILE
Social Competence—Boys Aged 4-5, 6-11, 12-16

% ile	Ages 4-5	Ages 6-11	12-16	4-5	Ages 6-11	12-16	*	Ages 6-11	12-16	T Score
≥69	7.5-12.0	9.0-12.0	9.0-12.0	7.0-12.0	8.0-12.0 75	8.5-12.0		5.5-6.0	5.5-6.0	55
	7.0	8.5	8.5	6.5	7.0	8.0		5.0	5.0	
50	6.5	8.0	8.0	6.0	6.5	7.5 7.0				50
	6.0	7.5	7.5		6.0					
	5.5	7.0	7.0	5.5		6.5		4.5	4.5	45
31	5.0	6.5	6.5	5.0	5.5	6.0		4.0	4.0	
	4.5	6.0	6.0		5.0					40
16	4.0	5.5	5.5	4.5		5.5		3.5	3.5	
		5.0	5.0		4.5	5.0		3.0	3.0	35
	3.5	4.5	5.0	4.0	4.0					
7	3.0	4.0	4.5		3.5	4.5		2.5	2.5	
2	2.5	3.5	4.0 3.5			4.0				30
	2.0	3.0	3.0	3.5	3.0	3.5		2.0	2.0	25
		2.5	2.5	3.0	2.5	3.0		1.5	1.5	
	1.5	2.0	2.0	2.5	2.0	2.5				20
		1.5	1.5	2.0	1.5	2.0		1.0	1.0	
	1.0	1.0	1.0	1.5		1.5				15
				1.0	1.0	1.0		.5	.5	
	.5	.5	.5	.5	.5	.5				
	0	0	0	0	0	0		0	0	10

Normal Range

ACTIVITIES

___ I. A. # of sports
___   B. Mean of participation and skill in sports
___ II. A. # of nonsports activities
___   B. Mean of participation and skill in activities
___ IV. A. # of jobs
___   B. Mean job quality
___ Total

SOCIAL

___ III. A. # of organizations
___   B. Mean of participation in organizations
___ V. 1. # of friends
___   2. Frequency of contacts with friends
___ VI. A. Behavior with others
___   B. Behavior alone
___ Total

SCHOOL

___ VII. 1. Mean performance
___   2. Special class
___   3. Repeated grade
___   4. School problems
___ Total

*Not scored for 4-5-year-olds

Name ___
Case # ___
Age ___
Date CBCL filled out ___
CBCL filled out by ___
Sum of social competence scores ___
Sum I ___

Figure 2b. Profile used for boys to assess social competence on the Revised Child Behavior Profile. (Profile copyright 1982 by Thomas M. Achenbach and used by permission.)

factors appropriate for the child's sex and age group. The resulting behavior profile provides a clear graphic representation of that child's behavioral functioning in reference to a normative sample of the same sex and age group. Social competencies are calculated and represented in a similar fashion enabling the clinician to identify areas of behavioral strengths or areas that could be enhanced, for example, by encouraging participation in extracurricular activities.

Reliability and validity for the Child Behavior Checklist have been demonstrated to be quite acceptable.[4] Although the norms have been seen as limited[3], Achenbach's latest presentation of normative procedures[4] is thorough and well executed.

Achenbach asserts that multiple sources of data are necessary for a comprehensive behavioral assessment of children.[4] Accordingly, he has developed several scales to supplement the information obtained from the parent's rating form. A Teacher's Report Form[4] allows the child's teacher to report on the child's educational background, academically related adaptive skills, and behavior problems in the classroom. The Behavior Checklist portion resembles the parent's version, but several items are replaced or modified for relevance in the classroom.

A Direct Observation Form allows an experienced observer to obtain data in a number of school settings. Following a 10-minute observation period, the rater composes a narrative description of the behavior and then rates the observed behaviors on a 96-item checklist.

Also supplementing the parent's Child Behavior Checklist is the Youth Self-Report, designed for youngsters aged 11 to 18 years. Items can be read by the child or read aloud to him or her. The format of the Youth Self Report is similar to the Child Behavior Checklist but items are presented in the first person and modified for the self-report format.

Research concerning the reliability and validity of the supplementary scales is somewhat limited at present. Early impressions, however, indicate considerable clinical usefulness.[4]

The thorough empirical grounding of the Child Behavior Checklist and the availability of supplemental scales make it a highly useful instrument for assessing behavior problems in childhood.

CASE ILLUSTRATION

Billy P.'s mother completed the Child Behavior Checklist in the pediatrician's waiting room just before seeing the doctor for Billy's regular 4-year-old physical examination. Scoring was performed by office personnel while the doctor examined Billy and the Profile was made available for him to review as part of the interview with Mrs. P.

Although Billy's mother rated his behavior on externalizing items as within average limits for his age (T score = 57, i.e., within one standard deviation of the mean), her rating of internalizing items resulted in a score well above age expectations (T score = 72, i.e., more than 2 standard deviations above the mean). Analysis of specific factors indicated especially high scores on the Social Withdrawal and Depressed Scales. Review of the social competence portion of the checklist indicated few out-of-home activities.

When these issues were discussed with Mrs. P., she evidenced a limited knowledge of the emotional and social needs of young children. The pediatrician suggested that she return, along with Mr. P., for several sessions of child guidance counseling.

Behavior Problem Checklist

Quay and Peterson[12] developed a behavior rating scale for children 5 years to 12 years of age that inspired considerable research and clinical use.[13] The scale is based on Peterson's 1961 study of teacher-reported behavior problems.[14] The scale comprises 55 items descriptive of children's behavior problems. The child's parent or teacher rates each item on a three-point scale on the basis of his or her assessment of that item's severity. The child's total score on the scale is compared to the normative data to determine the presence of a significant behavior problem. Peterson's earlier factor analytic work on these items revealed two factors: Conduct Problems and Personality Problems.[14] Later studies[15] produced two other factors: Inadequacy–Immaturity and Socialized Delinquency.

Although the Behavior Problem Checklist has had considerable clinical use it has been the target of some specific criticisms. For example, it has been pointed out that although some items are quite specific and easily observed (e.g., "crying" and "thumbsucking"), other items require considerable inference on the part of the rater (e.g., "lack of self-confidence").[13] It has been noted also that this scale does not allow for the identification of any assets the child might possess.

The Quay-Peterson Behavior Problem Checklist has shown adequate reliability although agreement between raters seems to decrease for older children.[14] Normative data have been compiled[16] and the validity of the scale has been shown to be acceptable.[17]

The weaknesses of this scale are the ones typically found in behavior rating scales. Its worth is in its ability to screen children for behavior problems. As in the Conners' scales, rating error can be overcome through brief training experiences.

References

1. Achenbach TM: The classification of children's psychiatric symptoms: A factor analytic study. *Psychol Monographs* 80, 1966.
2. Achenbach TM, Edelbroch CS: The classification of child psychopathology: A review and analysis of empirical efforts. *Psychol Bull* 85:1275–1301, 1978.
3. Sattler JM: *Assessment of Children's Intelligence and Special Abilities*, ed 2. Boston, Allyn & Bacon Inc, 1982.
4. Achenbach TM, Edelbrock CS: *Manual for the Child Behavior Checklist and Revised Child Behavior Profile*. Burlington, VT, Thomas M. Achenbach, 1983.
5. Conners CK: Symptom patterns in hyperkinetic, neurotic, and normal children. *Child Dev* 41:667–682, 1970.
6. Conners CK: A teacher rating scale for use in drug studies with children. *Am J Psych* 126:884–888, 1969.
7. Sprague RL, Cohen M, Werry JS: *Normative Data on the Conners' Teacher Rating Scale and Abbreviated Scale*. Technical Report, Children's Research Center, University of Illinois, Urbana, 1974.
8. Kupietz S, Bialer I, Winsberg BG: A behavior rating scale for assessing improvement in behaviorally deviant children: A preliminary investigation. *Am J Psych* 128:116–120, 1972.
9. Sprague RL, Christensen DE, Werry JS: Experimental psychology and stimulant drugs, in Conners CK (ed): *Clinical Use of Stimulant Drugs in Children*. The Hague, Excerpta Medica, 1974.
10. Ross DM, Ross SA: *Hyperactivity: Research, Theory, and Action*, New York, John Wiley & Sons, 1976, p 313.
11. Goyette CH, Conners, CK, Ulrich RF: Normative data on revised Conners' Parent and Teacher Rating Scales. *J Abnorm Child Psychol* 6:221–236, 1978.
12. Quay HC, Peterson DR: *Manual for the Behavior Problem Checklist*. Champaign, Ill, Children's Research Center, University of Illinois, 1967.
13. Ciminero AR, Crabman, RS: Current developments in the behavioral assessment of ' children, in Lahey BB, Kazdin AE (eds) *Advances in Clinical Child Psychology*. New York, Plenum Press, 1977, Vol 1.
14. Peterson DR: Behavior problems of middle childhood. *J Consult Psychol* 25:205–209, 1961.
15. Quay HC: Measuring dimensions of deviant behavior: The Behavior Problem Checklist. *J Abnorm Child Psychol* 5:277, 1977.
16. Werry JC, Quay HC: The prevalence of behavior symptoms in younger elementary school children. *Am J Orthopsych* 41:136–143, 1971.
17. Speer DC: The behavior problem checklist: Baseline data from parents of child guidance and nonclinic children. *J Consult Clin Psychol* 36:221–228, 1971.

Chapter 6

Screening Instruments

Screening procedures provide rapid, rough approximations of functioning in one or more potential problem areas for a child and offer hypotheses, when results are positive, which can be followed up with more definitive diagnostic assessment. Although some other tests in this book could at times be considered within the realm of screening instruments, the several methods described in this chapter are generally accepted screening measures which rapidly ascertain, in a global fashion, current levels of functioning and measure acquired skills in comparison to developmental norms. Screening instruments do not attempt to delineate a child's particular strengths and weaknesses. Furthermore, they are not justifiably used in making important educational or clinical decisions. The Denver Developmental Screening Test (DDST), the Developmental Screening Inventory (DSI), the Draw-A-Person technique, the Peabody Picture Vocabulary Test (PPVT), and the Slosson Intelligence Test are all examples of what are typically regarded as screening devices.

The DDST and the DSI are both simple methods of evaluating infants and young children by using primarily observations and/or parent reporting. Both instruments attempt to estimate the level of development of several abilities (fine and gross motor, language, personal and social), but the DSI ends at 36 months whereas the age limit of the DDST extends through the preschool years.

Human figure drawings were initially developed as quick estimates of intellectual maturity. There is much evidence to support the impression that drawings relate to the child's developmental milestones and that drawings can be considered as part of an implicit rule system. Later modifications in the instructions for the use of drawings focused on their potential as personality correlates as well as measures of intellectual maturity.

The PPVT is also used as a rough estimate of intellectual functioning, although it is limited to assessing receptive language skills. It is particularly helpful when testing children who are nonverbal or who have expressive language problems without hearing impairment.

The final test to be discussed here deals with an abridged form of a more familiar IQ test. The Slosson Intelligence Test is merely a shortened version of a combined Stanford-Binet and Gesell Child Development Behavior Inventory. Like all screening devices, its main advantages are its ease in administration and its quick delivery time.

Denver Developmental Screening Test

The Denver Developmental Screening Test (DDST) is used to identify developmental delays in children from birth through 6 years of age.[1,2] Because the DDST is a screening measure, it should not be used for diagnostic purposes. Rather, significant developmental delays identified with the DDST must be substantiated with further, more thorough, and valid testing (e.g., the Bayley Scales of Infant Development for children 2 to 30 months [see Chapter 7]; the Stanford-Binet for children 2 years and above [see Chapter 7]).

The DDST assesses a youngster's development in four areas: personal-social, fine motor, gross motor, and language (see Figures 3a,b). The personal-social area focuses on a child's self-help and early social skills. The fine motor area evaluates a child's finger manipulations and the drawing of simple shapes. Gross motor tests assess general body control with emphasis on coordination and balance. The language portion tests the child's receptive and expressive language skills. Test kits, forms, training manuals, and films can be obtained from the publisher (LADOCA Publishing Foundation, Denver, Colorado, 80216).

The DDST is designed for screening children from birth to 6 years, although it is especially useful for screening children aged 3 months to 4 years. It is inexpensive as well as easy and quick to administer (requiring about 20 minutes to administer and score). Because no formal training or experience is necessary, the DDST is frequently employed in health clinics, pediatricians' offices, and preschools.

1. Try to get child to smile by smiling, talking or waving to him. Do not touch him.
2. When child is playing with toy, pull it away from him. Pass if he resists.
3. Child does not have to be able to tie shoes or button in the back.
4. Move yarn slowly in an arc from one side to the other, about 6" above child's face. Pass if eyes follow 90° to midline. (Past midline; 180°)
5. Pass if child grasps rattle when it is touched to the backs or tips of fingers.
6. Pass if child continues to look where yarn disappeared or tries to see where it went. Yarn should be dropped quickly from sight from tester's hand without arm movement.
7. Pass if child picks up raisin with any part of thumb and a finger.
8. Pass if child picks up raisin with the ends of thumb and index finger using an over hand approach.

9. Pass any enclosed form. Fail continuous round motions.
10. Which line is longer? (Not bigger.) Turn paper upside down and repeat. (3/3 or 5/6)
11. Pass any crossing lines.
12. Have child copy first. If failed, demonstrate

When giving items 9, 11 and 12, do not name the forms. Do not demonstrate 9 and 11.

13. When scoring, each pair (2 arms, 2 legs, etc.) counts as one part.
14. Point to picture and have child name it. (No credit is given for sounds only.)

15. Tell child to: Give block to Mommie; put block on table; put block on floor. Pass 2 of 3. (Do not help child by pointing, moving head or eyes.)
16. Ask child: What do you do when you are cold? ..hungry? ..tired? Pass 2 of 3.
17. Tell child to: Put block on table; under table; in front of chair, behind chair. Pass 3 of 4. (Do not help child by pointing, moving head or eyes.)
18. Ask child: If fire is hot, ice is ?; Mother is a woman, Dad is a ?; a horse is big, a mouse is ?. Pass 2 of 3.
19. Ask child: What is a ball? ..lake? ..desk? ..house? ..banana? ..curtain? ..ceiling? ..hedge? ..pavement? Pass if defined in terms of use, shape, what it is made of or general category (such as banana is fruit, not just yellow). Pass 6 of 9.
20. Ask child: What is a spoon made of? ..a shoe made of? ..a door made of? (No other objects may be substituted.) Pass 3 of 3.
21. When placed on stomach, child lifts chest off table with support of forearms and/or hands.
22. When child is on back, grasp his hands and pull him to sitting. Pass if head does not hang back.
23. Child may use wall or rail only, not crawl.
24. Child must throw ball overhand 3 feet to within arm's reach of tester.
25. Child must perform standing broad jump over width of test sheet. (8-1/2 inches)
26. Tell child to walk forward,  heel within 1 inch of toe. Tester may demonstrate. Child must walk 4 consecutive steps, 2 out of 3 trials.
27. Bounce ball to child who should stand 3 feet away from tester. Child must catch ball with hands, not arms, 2 out of 3 trials.
28. Tell child to walk backward, ← toe within 1 inch of heel. Tester may demonstrate. Child must walk 4 consecutive steps, 2 out of 3 trials.

<u>DATE AND BEHAVIORAL OBSERVATIONS</u> (how child feels at time of test, relation to tester, attention span, verbal behavior, self-confidence, etc,):

Figure 3a. The Denver Developmental Screening Test—Revised, directions. (Copyright 1978 by W. K. Frankenburg, MD and used by permission.)

The DDST is individually administered. Items appropriate for the child's chronological age are presented according to simple, standardized directions. Each item is scored objectively as a pass or a fail. Passing an item means that the child being tested can perform that behavior which is defined as a skill or behavior performed by 90% of

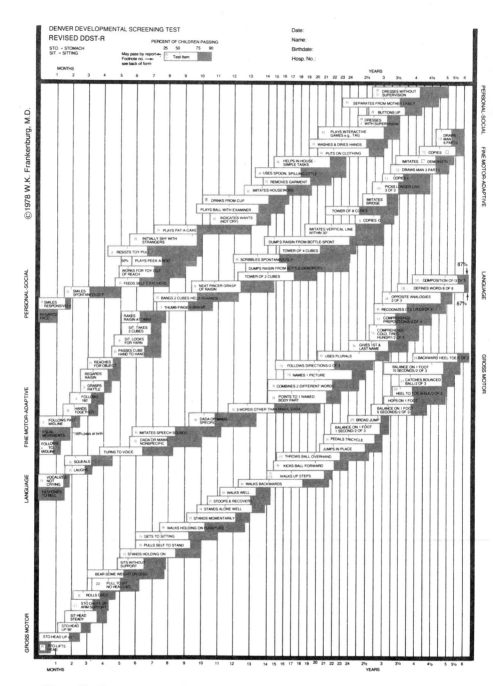

Figure 3b. The DDST-Revised. (Copyright 1978 by W. K. Frankenburg, MD and used by permission.)

the normative group younger than the child. Total test results are then judged as "normal," "questionable," or "abnormal" according to the number of failed or untestable items within the four broad areas.

The test–retest and interrater reliability coefficients for the DDST have been somewhat low but acceptable.[2] Correlations between the DDST and accepted measures of intelligence indicate high degrees of agreement.[2] Typical of screening tests, the DDST produces a number of overreferrals (approximately 7% that turn out to have no developmental problems). Of more concern, however, is the DDST's inability to identify consistently preschool and primary students with significant neurological and/or neurodevelopmental disorders.[3]

A more recent abbreviated and revised version of the DDST[4] is available to shorten the administration time. The revision also permits the clinician to assess more easily the child's development across time. Also available is the Denver Prescreening Developmental Questionnaire (PDQ)[5] which takes 97 of the 105 DDST items and formulates them into questions that can be answered by the child's parent or primary caretaker. At any age the parent responds to only 10 questions. Nine or 10 passes signifies normal development and no need for more thorough assessment. Six or fewer passes indicate a need for the full DDST (and subsequent referral for a more thorough assessment if the full DDST shows delays). Seven or eight passes indicate a need for the PDQ to be repeated one month later to rule out temporary lags in development.

Problems identified in using the DDST include the above mentioned "missing" of some neurologically impaired children and a somewhat socioeconomically unrepresentative standardization sample.[6] These concerns have led some reviewers to caution against its use as a screening instrument.[7(p 276)] Although the DDST is widely used, the Developmental Screening Inventory (see next section) also enjoys considerable popularity.

CASE ILLUSTRATION

Jennifer is a 3-year-old girl seen by her pediatrician for a well checkup. Jennifer's mother expressed concerns about Jennifer's speech development and as a result the Denver Developmental Screening Test was administered. Jennifer passed all of the items in the Personal-Social, Fine-Motor, and Gross-Motor areas but was delayed on four of six items administered in the language area. The pediatrician discussed these findings with Jennifer's mother, who agreed to a referral to a clinical child psychologist. The results of that evaluation substantiated the presence of an expressive language delay in the context of above average overall cognitive skills

*and average receptive language skills. Further referral was made
to a speech-language therapist.*

Developmental Screening Inventory

The Developmental Screening Inventory (DSI)[8] is used to establish
a child's current developmental status and screen for the presence of
developmental delays. The DSI is based on the Gesell Developmental
Schedules[9] developed by pediatrician Arnold Gesell and his associates
in the 1920s and 1930s. From observations of a sample of 107 normal,
white, "middle-class" infants, Gesell was able to determine the emer-
gence of predictable patterns of developmentally based behaviors. The
original DSI appeared in Gesell and Amatruda's text, *Developmental
Diagnosis,*[8] and was recently updated and published as the Revised
Developmental Screening Inventory.[10] The basic manual remains the
Developmental Diagnosis text.

The DSI screens development in five areas: Adaptive (sensorimotor and problem-solving antecedents of intelligence), Gross Motor,
Fine Motor, Language, and Personal-Social. Representative items from
each area appear at discrete age levels through the scale: at four-week
intervals through 1 year of age, at three-month intervals from 1 to 2
years of age, and at six-month intervals to 3 years of age. The placement
of items was based on normative research so that 50% of "normal"
infants would achieve success at that age level.

The DSI is used in pediatricians' offices, clinics, and hospitals.
Although no formal training is required, the examiner should have
experience with infants and young children and familiarity with the
DSI manual and materials.

The administration of the DSI requires a flat surface on which the
child can display motor behaviors, a table surface for manipulation of
test objects, and test objects (easily purchased or obtained) including
an embroidery hoop, small cup, 10 one-inch wooden cubes, crayon,
book, and small toy. Developmental accomplishments are judged from
behaviors observed during the course of the evaluation, behaviors elic-
ited by the presentation of test objects, and/or from a developmental
history obtained from the child's parent or major caretaker. The actual
administration procedures and scoring rules are presented in the manual.

Items are scored as pass (+) or fail (−). Testing begins at the
chronological age of the child and continues in each developmental
area until there are no passes at two consecutive age levels. Order of
presentation is influenced by Gesell's idea that a child should be given

the opportunity to show more sophisticated behavior first (e.g., the child should be given a chance to name an item before being asked to point to it).

Gesell's original intention was that his developmental schedules should be used as guides for clinical evaluation, with qualitative descriptions rather than numerical scores preferred in reporting the child's performance on the schedules. However, a developmental quotient (DQ) can be calculated for each of the five areas of development by computing a development age (based on a child's highest successes in that area), dividing by chronological age, and multiplying by 100 [DQ = (DA/CA) × 100]. DQs less than 70 suggest abnormal functioning in that area and the need for more thorough testing.

The DSI is appropriate for handicapped children, although it is important to understand how the handicap may influence the child's developmental patterns. Scoring, although intended to be objective, frequently requires subjective decisions on the part of the examiner. As with all procedures for use with infants and young children, the child's fatigue, distractibility, and comfort with the examiner must be considered when interpreting the test results.

The statistical reliability and validity of the Gesell Schedules and DSI have been studied extensively. A review by Thomas[11] indicated that appropriately trained examiners obtain high interrater *reliabilities*. However, Thomas's review showed less impressive *validity*. Although accurate predictions about later development of severely impaired infants could be made, the DSI showed less predictive power for other infants than the more thorough infant intelligence tests (viz., the Bayley Scales of Infant Development, see Chapter 7). It was also noted in Thomas's review that the normative data were insufficient for quantitative conclusions making qualitative description more preferable.

In the final analysis, the DSI's greatest value lies in its establishment of developmental benchmarks for guiding clinical impressions of a child's functioning. It has been noted that for purposes of screening for developmental delays the Denver Developmental Screening Test is superior.[12]

Goodenough-Harris Drawing Test

The Goodenough-Harris Drawing Test,[13] more commonly called the Draw-A-Person Test or Human Figure Drawing, is a brief, screening device which can be used as an estimate of intelligence for school-age children. It is appealing to children, easily administered and scored, and quite reliable.[14] Often the same drawing can be used for projective inferences (see "House-Tree-Person and Family Drawings" in Chapter 11).

The objective in this technique is to assess cognitive maturation and is based on Goodenough's[15] conjecture that an estimate of early school-age children's intelligence can be derived from their attempts at drawing a person. A child usually begins to draw identifiable figures somewhere around three or four years of age.[16] These drawings of persons are typically very primitive, for instance, having a head with minimal facial features with the remaining parts of the body stemming from the face. Often the head and body are drawn together as one circular shape. With ongoing development, the child's drawing of a person becomes increasingly more heterogenous and exact.

Directions for administering the test are relatively easy. The child is usually asked to construct three figures, a person, then another person of the opposite sex, and finally a self-portrait, which is used mainly for projective inferences. In each drawing the child is instructed to make each person as complete as possible, that is, more than merely the head and shoulders. No time constraints are required since the examiner is attempting to discover the child's total knowledge concerning human body parts. Unlike interpretations concerned with psychodynamics, the Goodenough-Harris method strives for the best figure that the child is able to produce.[16]

The scoring of the drawing focuses on its detail and complexity and primarily taps visual-motor coordination and concept formation abilities. It may also be instrumental in more complex functions since it has been found to be correlated with social adjustment.[17] IQs derived from the scoring correlate fairly well with the Stanford-Binet and even better with the Wechsler Scales, although the drawing IQ is usually lower than the scores from these more complete tests.[7] Thus, the Draw-A-Person Test should not be a substitute for more comprehensive tests of intelligence.

The actual scoring method is specific and elaborate. A total of 73 items (71 for the female figure) are scored on a pass–fail basis depending upon the appearance or nonappearance of body parts or particular items (e.g., arm movement) and on the adequacy of composition (e.g., lines in the drawing). If the child's attempts are just purposeless and uncontrolled scribbles, the score would be zero (which is equivalent to 3 years, 0 months). Any detail which appears to have direction or some purpose is given one point. Each point is based on three-month intervals. The scoring guide gives credit or no credit for such features as presence of head, trunk, legs, and arms, attachment of arms and legs, presence of eyes, nose, mouth, and hair, details of fingers, and accurate proportions of the features.

The obtained point total can be transformed to standard scores for the male and female drawings. Separate normative tables from age 3 to 15 for each of the two figures have been constructed for boys and girls separately (no norms have been provided for the self-drawing, which is more similar to a projective technique). The average standard score is 100 with a standard deviation of 15 (similar to the Wechsler Scales). The standard score can also be converted to a percentile rank. Alternately, age equivalents can be calculated using number of points earned.

Koppitz[18] has also constructed a scoring method for obtaining cognitive maturity based on a child's drawing. However, it has been criticized as being too general in comparison to the specific numerical values offered by the Harris tables.[16] For each drawing, the Koppitz system describes the number of items "expected," "common," "not unusual," or "exceptional" for the child's age. The main conclusion derived using this system is that the child's drawing is typical of a child of a particular age. These general comments concerning what portions of the body can be expected from a child at a certain age group are justifiable in relation to the degree of refinement offered by drawing a human figure.[16]

CASE ILLUSTRATION

The stick figure (Figure 4) was drawn by a girl 5 years and 10 months old who was referred for psychological testing by her pediatrician to assess her cognitive maturity. The drawing was scored for its inclusion of body parts (arms and legs and their attachment, head with sufficient space left for chin and forehead, trunk, eyes, mouth) and hair. A total of nine points equaled a standard score of 76 with a percentile rank of 9, suggesting functioning at approximately one and one-half standard deviations below the mean.

The second drawing (Figure 5) was completed by a child 6 years and 3 months old referred by school officials because of behavioral and academic problems. Fifteen points were scored for the presence of a head with sufficient space left for chin and forehead, trunk, shoulders (two points), arms and legs and their attachments and correct proportion, neck (two points), eyes, nose, and mouth. This was equivalent to a standard score of 91 and percentile rank of 27, suggesting an estimate of somewhat below average intellectual functioning.

Figure 4. Drawing by a child 5 years, 10 months old.

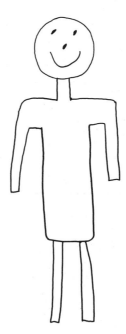

Figure 5. Drawing by a child 6 years, 3 months old.

Peabody Picture Vocabulary Test—Revised

The Peabody Picture Vocabulary Test—Revised (PPVT–R),[19] as well as its predecessor,[20] is an individually administered test designed to provide an estimate of verbal intelligence through receptive vocabulary. In this kind of test, the child is merely asked to identify, by whatever means, the one picture of four visually presented per page which best corresponds to the stimulus word spoken by the examiner. The PPVT–R is used with children from ages 2½ years through 18 years. Besides its use for presumably normal populations, it was also developed for use with special groups for whom standard tests were not always helpful in assessing receptive language (e.g., cerebral-palsied, brain-damaged, speech-defective, or emotionally withdrawn children and children with reading problems). Thus, this instrument has become an invaluable tool for the physician and psychologist whenever a question of developmental delay is present.

The PPVT–R is a simple test to administer and score with minimal specialized preparation required by the examiner beyond proper pronunciation of the stimulus words. It is an untimed individual test which is usually completed in 15 minutes or less. There is no special equipment needed other than the two forms, L and M, with 175 plates in

Figure 6. Training Plate A from the PPVT–R. (Reprinted from the Peabody Picture Vocabulary Test—Revised, by Lloyd M. Dunn and Leota M. Dunn, American Guidance Service, 1981.)

each form (four pictures to a plate; see Figure 6), an answer sheet, and a pencil. The answer sheet contains the stimulus word for each plate, the correct response number of the picture, and a space for recording the individual's responses. The reverse side of the answer sheet contains space for identifying information and for recording behavioral observations.

The manual states that the examiner must not spell, define, or show the stimulus word to the individual taking the test. The pictures have been shown to be attractive and interesting to the examinee, are clearly drawn, and present no problems with background interference.[7(p 270)] The manual suggests appropriate beginning points for different ages, a basal level (defined as the highest level at which the individual correctly responds to eight consecutive items), and a ceiling, or stopping point, at which six errors are made within any eight consecutive items. The final total or raw score is the number of correct pictures identified between the basal and ceiling levels. The raw score is then converted to a standard score, with an average of 100 and standard deviation of 15.

In obtaining items for the original test, the author stated that care was taken in selecting a "good cross section" of unbiased common words used in the United States. It is interesting to note, though, that only 111 of the original 300 pictures (37 percent) were included in the 1981 revision. In updating the test, item analyses procedures, which have been viewed as excellent, were instituted in the process to obtain new pictures.[7(p 270)] Pictures from the original edition discovered either to be culturally, sexually, racially, or regionally biased were deleted. The newer item selection includes a moderately well balanced combination of word pictures framed within 19 content categories.

The PPVT–R is also a significant improvement over its predecessor in regard to standardization. Whereas the original normative group was quite limited by its restricted geographical and racial makeup (4,012 white persons residing in or around Nashville, Tennessee), the revised edition offers a representative sample of 4,200 children stratified by geographical region, race, sex, community size, and occupation of primary wage earner. This improvement alone justifies the use of this version of the test and presents serious questions regarding the generalization of past results.

The PPVT–R has served often as a screening device for overall intellectual functioning. The assessor must remember, though, that he or she is tapping only a restricted portion of intellectual functioning (i.e., hearing vocabulary or receptive knowledge of vocabulary), and the results may not be consistent with the youngster's verbal output, visual-motor skills, or overall intellectual functioning.[21]

The obtained scores should not be viewed as an isolated IQ score or as a sole measure of language ability. The final score does not replace an IQ score obtained from a more complete intellectual battery. This is most apparent in samples of minorities where the PPVT has consistently yielded lower IQs than the Stanford-Binet.[7(p 270)] One examiner's experience[16(p 357)] has shown that the PPVT gave artificially high IQ scores for children whose parents tended to be articulate and well-educated. When the situation was reversed, it appeared that lower IQs were registered.

Slosson Intelligence Test

The Slosson Intelligence Test[22] is a brief individual test of intelligence designed to provide screening information on individuals from infancy through adulthood. The Slosson assesses mental ages from two weeks through 26 years with an item content derived from the Stanford-Binet[23] and the Gesell Developmental Schedules.[24] The test questions emphasize mathematical reasoning, vocabulary, auditory memory, and information. The main advantages of the Slosson are its ease and quickness of administration and its objective scoring system.[25]

The test questions are presented sequentially in ascending difficulty with each question labeled according to an age level which the average child should pass successfully. Although 194 questions comprise the test, a much smaller percentage is usually presented to the examinee.[16(p 354)] As in the Stanford-Binet, most questions require a verbal response, except for eight items in which geometric figures must be reproduced, and in the infant portion, where postural control and locomotion are assessed.

The administration of the test begins at the child's chronological age level. Exceptions are made in cases wherein the examiner anticipates lower or higher functioning from the child. For example, if a 6-year-old child appears brighter than normal, the examiner might begin testing at an 8-year-old level. A basal level is established by counting the highest in a series of ten correct answers. As questions progressively become more difficult, the examiner concludes testing at a ceiling level of ten failed answers in succession.

Scoring is expressed in age-months. Credit is granted by one-half month credits during year 1; by one month credits during years 2–4;

by two months credits during years 5–15; and by three months credits during years 16–26. A Mental Age is calculated by totaling the credited months. An estimated IQ score can then be made by dividing the mental age in months by the chronological age and multiplying by 100.

This manner of calculating an IQ score (called a ratio IQ) has a serious drawback in that the standard deviations differ greatly throughout the age ranges, thus limiting comparisons. Another serious liability of the test is its emphasis on language skills, which makes the test less useful for ages 2 to 3, especially when language has been delayed or when middle-class verbal patterns are not stressed by the child or parents.[25] A more salient criticism occurs at the earliest ages, when behavior is not well-represented due to a smaller sample of items.[7(p 244)] In this section of the test below age 2, the progression in items differs from the ordering on the much more widely accepted Bayley Scales of Infant Development.

The manual of the test also has serious deficiencies.[26] Demographic data from the standardization sample is not included. In fact, the sample is not well-described except as children and adults from rural and urban New York State. The test construction is described in only 25 lines, and only items providing favorable results are included. Finally, the manual includes anonymous testimonials which decrease the value of the appraisals offered.

Despite these criticisms, the Slosson correlates very highly with the Stanford-Binet, especially for ages 4–17.[16(p 354)] As a screening device, its main use comes when time is limited and major educational decisions (which are more appropriately made by non–screening tests) are not being considered. It can be used by school teachers, counselors, or health professionals in selecting individuals for more comprehensive evaluations of mental abilities. Because the time spent with the child is brief (approximately 15–20 minutes), the Slosson does not provide the more detailed information necessary to delineate cognitive strengths and weaknesses that more comprehensive tests of intelligence provide.

References

1. Frankenburg WK, Dodds JB: The Denver Developmental Screening Test. *J Pediatrics* 71:181–191, 1967.
2. Frankenburg WK, Dodds JB, Fandel AW, Kazuk E, Cohrs M: *Denver Developmental Screening Test: Reference Manual.* Denver, LADOCA Project and Publishing Foundation, 1975.
3. Sterling HM, Sterling PJ: Experiences with the QNST [Quick Neurological Screening Test]. *Academic Therapy* 12:339–342, 1977.

4. Frankenburg WK, Fandal AW, Sciarilo W, Burgess D: The newly abbreviated and revised Denver Developmental Screening Test. *J Pediatrics* 99:995–999, 1981.

5. Frankenburg WK, van Doorninck WJ, Liddell TN, Dick NP: The Denver Prescreening Developmental Questionnaire (PDQ). *Pediatrics* 57:774–753, 1976.

6. Werner EE: Review of the Denver Developmental Screening Test, in Buros OK (ed): *The Seventh Mental Measurements Yearbook.* Highland Park, NJ, Gryphon Press, 1972, pp 734–736.

7. Sattler JM: *Assessment of Children's Intelligence and Special Abilities,* ed 2. Boston, Allyn & Bacon Inc, 1982.

8. Gesell A, Amatruda CS: *Developmental Diagnosis.* New York, Paul B. Hoeber, 1947.

9. Gesell A et al: *Gesell Developmental Schedules.* New York, Psychological Corp, 1949.

10. Knobloch H, Stevens F, Malone AF: *The Revised Developmental Screening Inventory.* Albany, NY, New York State Office of Mental Retardation and Developmental Disabilities, 1980.

11. Thomas H: Psychological assessment instruments for use with human infants. *Merrill-Palmer Quarterly* 16:179–223, 1970.

12. Wright L, Schaefer AB, Solomons G: *Encyclopedia of Pediatric Psychology.* Baltimore, University Park Press, 1979.

13. Harris DB: *Children's Drawings as Measures of Intellectual Maturity: A Revision and Extension of the Goodenough Draw-A-Man Test.* New York, Harcourt, Brace & World, 1963.

14. Palmer JO: *The Psychological Assessment of Children.* New York, Wiley, 1970.

15. Goodenough FL: *Measurement of Intelligence in Children.* New York, World Book, 1926.

16. Gardner RA: *The Objective Diagnosis of Minimal Brain Dysfunction.* Cresskill, NJ, Creative Therapeutics, 1979.

17. Ochs E: *Changes in Goodenough Drawings associated with changes in social adjustment. J Clinical Psychology* 6:282–284, 1960.

18. Koppitz EM: *Psychological Evaluation of Children's Human Figure Drawings.* New York, Grune & Stratton, 1968.

19. Dunn LM, Dunn LM: *Peabody Picture Vocabulary Test—Revised.* Circle Pines, MI, American Guidance Services, 1981.

20. Dunn, LM: *Peabody Picture Vocabulary Test.* Circle Pines, MI, American Guidance Services, 1965.

21. Salvia J, Ysseldyke JE: *Assessment in Special and Remedial Education.* Boston, Houghton Mifflin, 1978, p 250.

22. Slosson RL: *Slosson Intelligence Test (SIT) for Children.* New York, Slosson Educational Publications, 1963.

23. Terman LM, Merrill MA: *Stanford-Binet Intelligence Scale.* Boston, Houghton-Mifflin, 1960.

24. Ilg, FL, Ames LB: *School Readiness: Behavior Tests Used at the Gesell Institute.* New York, Harper & Row, 1965.

25. Hunt JV: Review of the Slosson Intelligence Test, in Buros OK (ed): *Seventh Mental Measurements Yearbook.* Highland Park, NJ, Gryphon Press, 1972, p 424.

26. Himelstein P: Review of the Slosson Intelligence Test, in Buros OK (ed): *Seventh Mental Measurements Yearbook.* Highland Park, NJ, Gryphon Press, 1972, p 424.

Chapter 7

Cognitive Measures

Cognitive Measures

Broadly speaking, intelligence testing attempts to measure an individual's mental capacity, that is, his or her ability to understand and to cope with his or her world. There are more precise definitions of intelligence, but disagreements among theoreticians regarding the exact nature of intelligence continue to exist. For example, the question remains whether intelligence is comprised of a number of independent factors or one single factor or ability (general intelligence).[1]

Regardless of theoretical position, a sound intelligence test must meet the goals of adequate standardization, reliability, and validity.[1] In preparation, the test's items must have been presented to a wide variety of people of varying ages, geographical areas, and socioeconomic levels. To be reliable, the results of the test must be consistent from examiner to examiner and from one administration to another. For a test to be valid there must be evidence that it actually measures what it was designed to measure.

The following sections discuss several of the soundest and most widely used intelligence tests for children, as well as one the major use of which is with deaf and other handicapped children (Leiter International Performance Scale[2]) and one with a new and innovative approach to the measurement of intelligence (Kaufman Assessment Battery for Children[3]). A number of other tests of children's intelligence are available. Information, including reviews, can be found in the standard source of information on tests, Buros's *Mental Measurement Yearbook*.[4]

Bayley Scales of Infant Development

The Bayley Scales of Infant Development are a well-standardized measure of development in infants and young children from 2 months to 30 months.[5] They are considered to be the best measure of infant development in terms of reliability, validity, and general usefulness and provide valuable data regarding early mental and motor development. They have considerable utility in identifying the presence of developmental delays. An initial administration of the Bayley Scales for a particular child provides a baseline against which later evaluations can be compared in order to assess rates of growth and development in the mental and motor areas. Prior to the Bayley, researchers and clinicians had to rely on infant tests with less rigorous standardization and less acceptable psychometric properties, such as the Cattell Infant Intelligence Scale.[6]

The Bayley Scales of Infant Development consist of three separate scales: a Mental Scale, a Motor Scale, and an Infant Behavior Record. The Mental Scale consists of 163 items arranged chronologically beginning at a 2-month level and ending at a 30-month level. In the earliest months the Mental Scale consists of measures of sensory intactness and efficiency including visual fixation and visual tracking as well as auditory awareness and localization. Later in the scale, a number of diverse activities and processes are assessed including purposeful manipulation of objects, visual discrimination, early language development, and memory.

The Motor Scale consists of 81 items (also arranged chronologically) that assess both fine and gross motor abilities. In the fine motor realm various steps in the process of locomotion are assessed such as rolling over, crawling, and walking with help.

Each mental and motor item is numbered and assigned two age markers: one for the average age at which the item is passed and a range (usually of several months) with which 95% of the children in the standardization sample passed that item. This age range is valuable in clarifying the variability that exists in normal children's developmental accomplishments.

The Mental Scale yields a Mental Development Index and the Motor Scale yields a Psychomotor Development Index. Both of these index scores have means of 100 and standard deviations of 16. Although not IQs, these scores have the same statistical properties for purposes of classification. An index score of less than 68 (more than 2 standard deviations below the mean) is considered deficient.

The Infant Behavior Record is not a formally administered portion of the Bayley Scales but rather a systematic way of observing and assessing several key behavioral and emotional features occurring during the examination. Ratings can be compared to the standardization group in 11 areas including social orientation, cooperation, fearfulness, tension, emotional tone, object orientation, goal directedness, attention span, endurance, activity, and reactivity. The Infant Behavior Record is useful in objectifying behavioral observations in these areas. Emotional and behavioral deviations at these early ages can be significant in terms of the child's emotional well-being. Other behaviors, including goal directedness, attention span, object orientation, and reactivity tend to be correlated positively with mental scores. The considerable interest that has been generated recently in the area of early infant behavior and infant mental health makes the Infant Behavior Record a valuable tool for the clinician interested in these issues.

The Bayley Scales of Infant Development require individual administration by a trained examiner familiar with the Bayley materials and manual. The examiner should be comfortable with and accustomed to being with infants and should be well versed in normal patterns of development. The test is used frequently in hospitals and child development clinics. Together, the mental and motor scales require approximately 45 minutes to administer. A small proportion of children may require an administration time of from 60 to 90 minutes. For children who have difficulty separating from the mother, it may be necessary to have the mother or primary caretaker present for the evaluation.

Although items are arranged chronologically, test items with similar content are administered consecutively. For example, manipulating one-inch cubes begins at a 3-month level with simple grasping and proceeds all through the test with increasing complexity including block stacking and arranging blocks into a train-like configuration. Testing is completed when a basal level and a ceiling level are obtained. On the mental scale, a basal is assumed when the infant has passed approximately ten consecutive items. All prior items are thus considered within the youngster's abilities. A ceiling occurs when an infant is unable to pass approximately ten items consecutively. All later items are considered too difficult for that particular youngster. The total number of items passed between the basal and ceiling is entered into the normative tables which consist of 14 age group ranges. The developmental index score is then determined.

Common administration problems include failure to develop adequate rapport with the infant and an inability to keep the child interested long enough to complete the testing. In addition, many children do not cooperate with some of the motor items. Handicapped infants may require items to be presented in ways that minimize any interference in performance that the handicap may pose. These administration problems are less common with well-experienced examiners. Although pass–fail criteria are clearly stated for each test item, actual judgments for certain items tend to be subjective.

The reliability coefficients for the various age groups for both the mental and motor scales are acceptable and fairly consistent throughout the age periods.[5,7 (p 254)] However, reliabilities for the motor scale tend to be lower for the first four months. The correlations between the mental and motor scales vary considerably and tend to decrease with age. This lack of agreement indicates that motor and mental development are different and should be assessed separately in this age group. Validity is more difficult to assess in that the Bayley Scales tend to be the best standardized of the infant assessment scales. A strong positive correlation exists between the Stanford-Binet and the Bayley Scales for the ages during which the scales overlap.[5] It should be emphasized that there is little or no continuity between the measures of early development and the measures of intelligence in school-aged children. That is, early developmental functioning has little predictive validity in terms of later intelligence. An exception is for youngsters who clearly fall within the deficient range on the Bayley Scales. These youngsters are likely impaired to some degree, and it is in the identification of these children that the Bayley Scales are most useful. Average or better scores on the Bayley Scales, especially within the first several months, may at best be an indication that the infant is intact.

The Bayley Scales are considered to be the very best measure of infant development.[8] Although their administration is difficult for the novice, in the hands of a well-experienced examiner they provide a wealth of information about an infant's development at a particular point in time and more importantly, an objective measure of any changes in an infant's development across time.

CASE ILLUSTRATION

Jason R., at 12 months, was referred for a psychological evaluation following his failing several items on the Denver Developmental Screening Test at the local health department. The local department of social services had been alerted to possible neglect and/or abuse and pursued the check-up at the health department.

When seen later by the psychologist, Jason appeared as a pale, thin child who cooperated passively and listlessly with the testing procedures. Although his attention was adequate for the purposes of the examination, he did not actively engage the examiner.

The results of the Bayley Scales of Infant Development showed deficient mental functioning, with a Mental Development Index of 65 (more than 2 standard deviations below the mean) and only slightly delayed motor functioning, with a Psychomotor Development Index of 85 (1 standard deviation below the mean). Among the Mental Scale items Jason's earliest failures occurred at the five-month and seven-month levels on tasks assessing interest in sound productions and early vocalizations. His highest pass was at the 11-month level on a task requiring pushing a toy car following a demonstration by the examiner. On motor tasks Jason passed virtually all items through the 11-month level. The difference between Jason's mental and motor development was statistically significant and was seen as probably reflecting inadequate stimulation.

Following the social service investigation it was found that Jason had been neglected and he was removed from his natural mother and placed temporarily in foster care. At 21 months he was reevaluated with the Bayley Scales. On this administration Jason seemed more active and engaging. He freely explored the testing room and comfortably approached the examiner. He enjoyed the testing procedures and cooperated fully. Results of testing reflected improvements in developmental functioning with an MDI of 80 and PDI of 90. The significant increase in his mental functioning was seen, in part, as a result of his more enriching environment. It was recommended that he be evaluated once again in a year in order to track his developmental functioning.

Stanford-Binet Intelligence Scale

The Stanford-Binet Intelligence Scale[9] enjoys a reputation as one of the oldest and most frequently used instruments for the measurement of intelligence.[7] The roots of the most recent revision of the Stanford-Binet can be traced directly back to 1905 when Alfred Binet, in collaboration with Theodore Simon, developed a method to separate mentally retarded from normal children in the Paris public schools. Early revisions of this original version appeared in 1908 and 1911. In 1908 test items were grouped according to age level and in 1911 test items were refined to measure intellect rather than academic achievement. When the test was brought to the United States, additional revisions proved necessary. The 1916 scale (the Stanford Revision and Extension of the Binet-Simon Intelligence Scale) involved considerable standardization efforts as well as the inclusion for the first time of a ratio of mental age and chronological age which was named the intelligence quotient (IQ). A significant revision was made in 1937 which featured better statistics and clinical usefulness. Finally, when the version used currently appeared in 1960, it abandoned the previously used ratio IQ in favor of a more statistically acceptable deviation IQ, a score based on an individual's functioning in comparison to the normative age group. In 1972 wider standardization and better normative procedures were established, along with minor revisions of some dated test items. A major revision was published in 1985[10] (see Figure 7). In addition to its popularity as a measure of intelligence, the Stanford-Binet (and its predecessor, the Binet-Simon Scale) has been credited with helping to stimulate the growth of clinical psychology in this country and elsewhere.[7]

As currently used, the Stanford-Binet provides a general measure of intellectual functioning in individuals from 2 years of age through adulthood. Test items are ordered chronologically in discrete age groupings. In its original conceptualization, the assumption was that an average individual could pass all of the tests through his or her own chronological age grouping. From ages 2 years to 6 years test items are grouped at six-month intervals, allowing for the rapid growth of intellectual development during this time. At age 6 years and beyond, test items

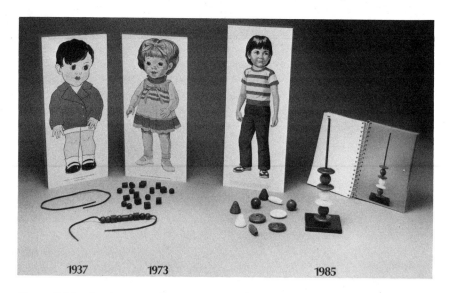

Figure 7. The development of two Stanford-Binet subtests. These materials are in the fourth edition. (Copyright 1985 by the Riverside Publishing Company and used by permission.)

are clustered at yearly intervals. At all age levels there are six tests, along with an alternative for "spoiled" tests (those that are not usable because of administration errors, for example). From ages 2 years to 6 years, each test item is credited as one month; from age 6 on, each test item is credited as two months.

The test items themselves tap a number of diverse verbal and nonverbal intellectual abilities including receptive and expressive language, short-term visual and auditory memory, verbal and nonverbal reasoning, and visual-spatial organization. Although many different intellectual skills are sampled throughout the scale, the scale's strength lies in providing a measure of general intellectual functioning. Specific functioning in a particular cognitive area is difficult to assess since the different abilities tested occur unevenly throughout the scale. For example, at the early age levels visual-spatial skills are tested more often than verbal ones; on the other hand, verbal processing tests predominate later in the scale. Examples of the tests, materials, and the abilities measured at ages two and six are provided below. Figure 8 shows materials from the 1972 edition of the Stanford-Binet.

Year Two

1. *Three-hole form board*: A 5-inch by 8-inch form board with three inserts for a circle, a square, and a triangle. To pass successfully, the child must place the three different shaped blocks in the proper holes. The test requires shape discrimination, visual-spatial organization, and fine motor manipulation.

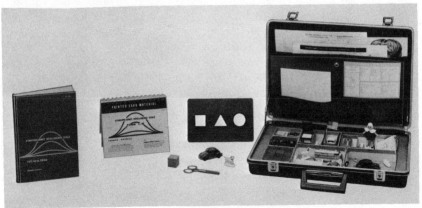

Figure 8. Test materials from the 1972 edition of the Stanford-Binet. (Copyright 1972 by the Riverside Publishing Company and used by permission.)

2. *Delayed response*: Three small cardboard boxes and a small toy cat. To pass successfully the child must remember (after a 10 second delay) in which of the three boxes the cat was hidden. This test involves attention, reasoning, and short-term visual recall.

3. *Identifying parts of the body*: A large paper doll. The child must identify the doll's hair, mouth, feet, ear, nose, hands, and eyes in response to the examiner's questions. The test requires single-word receptive vocabulary skills as well as an adequate acquired fund of information.

4. *Block building tower*: Twelve one-inch cubes. The child must build a tower of four or more blocks following the model built by the examiner. Successful performance requires visual-motor abilities and spatial awareness.

5. *Picture vocabulary*: Eighteen 2-inch by 4-inch cards, each with a picture of a common object. The child must name at least four successfully to pass at this age level. This test involves single-word expressive language, fund of information, and recall/verbal identification of familiar objects.

6. *Word combinations*: The child's spontaneous word combinations are noted and the child is credited if combinations of at least two words are uttered. This test taps expressive language skills.

Year Six

1. *Vocabulary*: A vocabulary card containing a list of words for the child to define, e.g., What is an apple? This test assesses a child's expressive language skills, verbal reasoning, and fund of information.

2. *Differences*: The child is asked what the difference is between two common items such as a fish and a cat. Successful performance involves abstract verbal reasoning and verbal expression.

3. *Mutilated pictures*: A card with altered pictures. The child must indicate what is gone in each picture. This test requires nonverbal reasoning and the perception of part–whole relationships.

4. *Number concepts*: Twelve one-inch cubes. To pass successfully the child must choose a designated number of blocks. This test requires numerical reasoning and rote counting ability.

5. *Opposite analogies II*: To pass successfully, the child must complete analogies such as, "A baby is small; a man is ———." The child must be able to engage in verbal conceptual reasoning.

6. *Maze tracing*: To pass successfully, the child must indicate the shortest way through several mazes. This test requires visual motor abilities, motor planning, and concentration.

The Stanford-Binet is individually administered and is appropriate for a wide variety of test purposes. Its most common and important function may still be in the assessment of mentally retarded individuals.[7] Physically handicapped children who are tested with this instrument should also be tested with other instruments in order to gain a more accurate picture of intellectual functioning since the handicapping condition may interfere with the youngster's ability to perform some of the required Stanford-Binet tasks. For example, a child with cerebral palsy would have difficulty with tests requiring motor manipulations. The Stanford-Binet is used in a variety of settings including schools, hospitals, and clinics. Reliable administration requires considerable education, training, and experience in testing children as well as familiarity with the manual and materials.

Testing proceeds from a basal level, which is defined as the last age grouping in which a youngster is able to perform all of the test items correctly, to a ceiling level, which is defined as the first age grouping in which a youngster is unable to pass any of the test items. A mental age is calculated based on the total number of months earned. Using a series of tables, the mental age and the child's chronological age are used to calculate an IQ score. This deviation IQ score has a mean of 100 and a standard deviation of 16. The scoring criteria are objective and clearly presented in the testing manual, as are explicit directions for standardized administration of the test items. The examination time involves 30 to 40 minutes for young children and approximately an hour for older children, adolescents, and adults.

There are "short form" versions of the Stanford-Binet that provide reliable and valid IQs. However, important information can be lost for the benefit of a gain in time. Therefore, it is not recommended that short forms be used for clinical purposes. The Stanford-Binet has been shown to have impressive reliability and validity. IQ scores for individuals are consistent from one administration to another. Also, IQ scores are significantly and positively correlated with scores obtained from other measures of general intelligence. In fact, the Stanford-Binet is frequently used as the criterion against which the validity of other tests is established. As with scores from other tests of intelligence (e.g., the WISC–R), the IQ scores of the Stanford-Binet predict with considerable accuracy later academic achievement for preschool and school-aged children.

In actual clinical use, the Stanford-Binet Intelligence Scale is especially valuable in assessing intellectual functioning in youngsters aged 2 to 4. Whereas other preschool measures of intelligence provide for a more thorough understanding of particular intellectual strengths and weaknesses, the Stanford-Binet Intelligence Scale produces a reliable and valid measure of general intellectual ability. Also, with older mentally retarded individuals, the Stanford-Binet Intelligence Scale provides a useful measure of current intellectual functioning and growth when administered across time. Among the drawbacks of this instrument is the heavy reliance on verbal tests and the uneven distribution of test items for various intellectual abilities. Therefore, it is difficult to gain a firm understanding of an individual's particular intellectual strengths and weaknesses. This shortcoming makes diagnoses of learning disabilities and weaknesses difficult and better accomplished with other test instruments, including the Wechsler Intelligence Scale for Children—Revised[11] or the McCarthy Scales of Children's Abilities.[12] Further, it has been noted that the Stanford-Binet is not appropriate for purposes of educational planning.[13]

Many of these criticisms are addressed in the major revision of the Stanford-Binet published in 1985.[10] This version provides separate standard scores for its four scales: verbal reasoning, quantitative reasoning, visual-spatial reasoning, and short-term memory. These scales and most of the test items are new, although some familiar test items have been retained and updated (see Figure 8). Other improvements in the 1985 version include the use of sophisticated psychometric techniques for test item development and standardization procedures. This revision appears to be a considerable improvement over previous ones, but it will be some time before its clinical and heuristic value can be established.

CASE ILLUSTRATION

Amy S., 4½ years old and white, was referred for psychological assessment by her pediatrician because of suspected developmental delays. Amy had failed a developmental screening inventory administered in the pediatrician's office. Amy is the older of two children; her younger brother shows no particular developmental difficulties. During formal testing, Amy was well behaved, polite, and attentive. She showed little frustration during difficult tasks and clearly enjoyed her successes on easier items. The examiner's praise and encouragement were welcomed with frequent smiles. On the basis of her performance on the Stanford-Binet Intelligence Scale, Amy was found to be functioning with mild mental retardation. She was able to pass all of the items at the 2-year level but began failing verbal items at the 2½-year level. At the 3 and 3½-year level, Amy failed all of the verbal items. Her only passes at the 3½-year level involved items requiring fine-motor manipulations. Amy failed all of the items at the 4-year level. Her obtained mental age of 3 years, 5 months resulted in an IQ score of 64, a score more than 2 standard deviations below the mean.

In an interview with Amy's parents, her social and adaptive skills were assessed with the Vineland Social Maturity Scale (see Chapter 10) at a similarly delayed level. Thus it appears that this youngster was functioning with significant developmental delays in all areas, with particular deficits in her verbal skills.

The results of the evaluation were shared with the referring physician with the recommendation that she become involved in her school's special education preschool program for the appropriate educational assessment, planning, and intervention.

The pediatrician and psychologist both participated in an interpretive interview with Mr. and Mrs. S. The results of the evaluation and the recommendations were discussed. Amy's parents' questions and concerns were addressed and it was agreed that the psychologist would meet with them in one month to check on their adjustment.

The Wechsler Scales (WISC–R and WPPSI)

Within the broader scope of a medical or psychological evaluation, an intellectual assessment, as measured by an IQ test, is crucial in delineating a final diagnosis and treatment plan. The intelligence test can be used to assess the degree of mental retardation, provide support for organic brain diseases, and discover relationships of failure or success on certain tests to help discover specific learning disabilities. Because of the variety of subtests which aid in delineating a child's strengths and weaknesses, the Wechsler Scales lend themselves readily to these kinds of assessment.

The revised Wechsler Intelligence Scale for Children (WISC–R),[11] used for children aged 6 through 16 years, and its downward extension, the Wechsler Preschool and Primary Scale of Intelligence (WPPSI),[14] used for younger children aged 4 to 6½, have been the most widely used tests of children's intelligence in recent years. The WISC–R and WPPSI are individually administered tests which require specially trained psychologists who are thoroughly familiar with the mechanics of the tests and their scoring procedures. Although portions of the tests might be appropriate for children younger or older than the age ranges covered by the tests, the items, materials, and procedures for administration were chosen for their suitabilty with children 4 to 16 years, and norms are provided only for these ages. Where the two instruments overlap or where the WISC–R merges with the adult version, the Wechsler Adult Intelligence Scale—Revised (WAIS-R),[15] the choice of scale is left to the discretion of the examiner.

The distinguishing feature between the Wechsler Scales and other previously developed individual tests of intelligence for children, for example, the Stanford-Binet (see previous section), is its total renunciation of the mental age (MA) construct as a primary measure of intellect. Another salient difference is that the test items are separated into two dominant categories, verbal and performance. Three resulting intelligence quotients (IQs) can then be calculated at test completion—a Verbal Scale IQ score, a Performance Scale IQ score, and an overall Full Scale IQ score. This division of scores is often advantageous in explicating a child's strengths and weaknesses to help in the diagnosis of learning disabilities and to aid in developing appropriate remedial treatment planning.

One of the most innovative characteristics in the standardization of the original WISC was that IQ scores were collected by comparing each child's test score with values earned by individuals within a single peer group.[16] The main benefit derived from this method was that a child's IQ score would not fluctuate from year to year unless his or her obtained test performance varied in comparison to same-aged children. For instance, on retesting, a child's score automatically provides him or her with an IQ standing which is relative to a current age group at each time of testing. Any significant changes in score over time can then be attributed to changes in the child and not to the organization of the test or to its standardization.

The resulting IQ standing represents a relative intelligence rating called a deviation IQ since it designates the degree by which an individual child deviates above or below the mean performance of similar-aged children. The deviation score also has the advantage of being readily translated into percentile ranks. An IQ of 100 was established as the average score for each age grouping, with the standard deviation set at 15 IQ points. In terms of classification ranges for the WISC–R, scores of 69 and below are considered mentally deficient; 70–79, borderline; 80–89, low average; 90–109, average; 110–119, high average or bright; 120–129, superior; and 130 and greater, very superior.

The WISC–R consists of 12 subtests, with two being used as alternates or for supplementary information. Within each of the subtests, the items are provided according to level of difficulty. The examiner starts with easier items and continues to administer the more difficult questions until the child fails a predetermined number of consecutive items. Each subtest raw score is converted into standard scores with a mean of 10 and a standard deviation of 3.

The WISC–R subtests measure the following:

1. *Verbal Scale*
   (a) *Information*. This subtest provides a broad sampling of the child's general fund of information reflecting his or her degree of environmental stimulation, amount of formal education, and cultural interest.
   (b) *Similarities*. This subtest requires abilities such as verbal concept formation (abstract thinking) and logical thinking.
   (c) *Arithmetic*. This subtest requires the knowledge of basic arithmetical operations and the ability to reason correctly. The ability to concentrate and attend to the required task is necessary for successful completion.
   (d) *Vocabulary*. This subtest of word knowledge corresponds highly to the child's experiences and education and taps a wide variety of cognitive functions such as memory, learning ability, concept formation, richness of ideas, and language development. It is generally considered an excellent estimate of intellectual ability and has been shown to be stable over time and resistant to neurological deficit and psychological disturbances.
   (e) *Comprehension*. This subtest assesses judgment and common sense dealing in such diverse issues as personal firstaid, interpersonal relations, and societal activities.
   (f) *Digit Span*. This is one of the two supplementary tests consisting of repetition of digits forward and backward. Successful completion includes the ability to retain several unrelated items in proper sequence in memory storage and, in regard to digits backward, the requirement of mental manipulation and reorganization.

2. *Performance Scale*
   (a) *Picture Completion*. This is a task in which the child must discover a missing element in an otherwise complete picture. It requires such capacities as differentiating the essential from the nonessential parts, concentration, and visual alertness.
   (b) *Picture Arrangement*. This subtest requires the child to arrange a series of pictures into a meaningful sequence. Abilities needed for successful resolution include interpretation of social situations and planning ability.
   (c) *Block Design*. This is a subtest in which the child must combine a number of colored blocks into a pattern which is shown on a card. Achievement on the subtest measures perceptual organization and spatial visualization abilities with

perceptual organization and spatial visualization abilities with emphasis on visual analysis and synthesis.

(d) *Object Assembly.* This subtest consists of jigsaw-like puzzles which must be solved within a specified time limit. It is a test of perceptual organization ability requiring the child to grasp a concrete pattern by anticipating the association among separate parts.

(e) *Coding.* This subtest consists of symbols (shapes or numbers) with a special mark associated with each symbol. The child is required to place within or below the symbol all appropriate corresponding marks within 120 seconds. The processes involved include visual-motor coordination, speed of mental operation, and short-term memory. The test also reflects associative learning and the ability to learn new material quickly.

(f) *Mazes.* This is the other supplementary test and entails eight mazes. It measures planning ability and perceptual organization. Speed and visual-motor control in conjunction with accuracy are prerequisites for success.

The rationale described for the WISC–R subtests is essentially applicable in discussing the 12 WPPSI subtests. Three subtests were developed specifically for the WPPSI. These include Animal House (instead of Coding), Geometric Design (replacing Picture Arrangement), and Sentences (replacing Digit Span). The remaining subtests have the same names and are similar to the WISC-R subtests. The only other difference is that Mazes is a regularly administered Performance subtest and a retest of the Animal House subtest is used as a supplementary test.

3. *WPPSI Subtests*

(a) *Animal House.* Requirements for this Performance subtest consist of placing a colored cylinder (house) in front of each respective animal. Such skills as memory, associative learning, attention span, finger and manual dexterity, and goal awareness are tapped by this task.

(b) *Geometric Design.* This subtest, which requires the child to copy shapes from line drawings, measures perceptual and visual-motor organization attributes. Low scores are a possible indication of developmental lags. High scores are particularly difficult to obtain because the motor dexterity required for success is associated with maturational constraints.

(c) *Sentences.* This is a supplementary test involving memory in which the child repeats a sentence immediately after oral presentation by the examiner. It measures short-term recall and attention.

The length of the Wechsler Scales is considerable, requiring approximately 60 to 75 minutes of administration time, and another 30 minutes to score the protocol. The amount of time may be too much for younger or handicapped children, for whom two test sessions may be needed for completion. Therefore, there have been many attempts to develop abbreviated versions of the scales.

Probably the most popular short form for screening purposes is the two-subtest combination.[7] The Vocabulary and Block Design subtests have been used in this manner because of their high correlation with the Full Scale IQ and their consistantly high reliabilities.

Although the short forms are pragmatic and save time, the obtained IQs are less stable than the Full Scale IQ, and important information regarding cognitive variability is lost. This reduction in information actually defeats the purpose of adequate evaluation, especially in the assessment of a retarded child. At best, an abbreviated version is a screening device; at worst, it can be an abuse of what the scale actually represents.

The Wechsler Scales are often interpreted on the basis of irregular patterns of scores obtained by the child.[7] This irregular pattern often reflects the child's uneven skill development and implies the need for further investigation. The two main approaches in the tests' interpretation include: (a) the discrepancy between the Verbal and Performance Scale scores and (b) the differences among the subtest scores, technically called profile analysis or "test scatter."

Significantly discrepant scores between the Verbal and Performance Scales may indicate for the child deficiencies or strengths in such areas as processing information or working under pressure. A child must have a difference of 12 points between his or her Verbal and Performance IQs in order for it to be statistically significant at the .05 level (15 points at the .01 level). Only when significance can be established do the findings become relevant for discussion. Any less difference could be attributed to many intervening factors, for example, measurement error, and should not be considered a major finding.

The purpose of profile analysis is to assess whether a child is more skillful in one particular area than in another. Profiles which have sharp inclines or declines may be associated with a child's specific strengths and weaknesses and may give hints to the clinician regarding the child's cognitive style and avenues for possible remediation.

Viewing factor scores from the WISC–R is another way of producing hypotheses concerning the interpretation of a child's profile of scores.[17] These factors (called Verbal Comprehension, Perceptual Organization, and Freedom from Distractibility) offer the clinician additional information in which to conceptualize a child's performance. This is done by combining scores on Arithmetic, Coding, and Digit Span and considering them as a separate entity—Freedom from Distractibility—from Verbal Comprehension (the remaining Verbal Scale subtests) and Perceptual Organization (the remaining Performance Scale subtests). The clinician can then compare this Freedom from Distractibility factor, which measures the ability to attend, concentrate, and remain undistracted, against the other two factors. For instance, an average Freedom from Distractibility score that is three scaled score points below the average of the other two factors scores would provide greater substantiation that the child might have an attentional deficit.

The conclusions based on interpretations of test results should always be considered in light of other historical information and background factors. Testing a child individually is very difficult from testing a child in a classroom where sensory stimulation is high. Thus, the hypotheses surrounding the observed behaviors and test scores must integrate all that is known about the particular child before an accurate description can be communicated and remedial interventions recommended.

CASE ILLUSTRATION

George P., 6 years, 10 months old, was referred for intellectual testing by his therapist to gain additional information regarding attentional deficits and learning difficulties. The request was initiated because of concern about the possibility of a specific reading disability. Another therapist had been treating George on a weekly basis for one year prior to this referral. Initial presenting problems included inappropriate expressions of anger and questions concerning whether his overactivity had an emotional or organic basis. A report from his therapist noted continuing progress in controlling anger outbursts, gains in verbal expression of feelings, and a satisfactory adjustment to first grade.

Results from previous psychological testing using the WPPSI completed 1½ years prior to the present evaluation displayed functioning in the average intellectual range, with minimal disparity between verbal and performance abilities. Strengths were shown on subtests measuring verbal concept formation and social judgment. *Apparent weaknesses were discovered on tests requiring abilities in vocabulary skills and nonverbal reasoning. Also, a high degree of distractability was observed as well as difficulties in visual-motor integration.*

On this administration of the WISC–R, George obtained a Verbal Scale score of 105, a Performance Scale score of 101, with a resulting Full Scale score of 102. This latter IQ score placed him within the average range of intellectual functioning. Although there was much consistency in overall IQ scores, there was evidence of marked differences among subtest scores.

The following scores on the subtests were noted:

Information	10	Picture Completion	7
Similarities	11	Picture Arrangement	14
Arithmetic	5	Block Design	10
Vocabulary	15	Object Assembly	12
Comprehension	13	Coding	8

As can be observed, George had developed some outstanding abilities. These included a broad knowledge of vocabulary skills and above average abilities in grasping social conventions and interpreting social situations. Combined, these skills implied that George had developed solid abilities in interpreting, using, and expressing factual societal information in a meaningful and emotionally relevant manner.

His weaker areas were displayed on tasks measuring numerical reasoning and accuracy, visual-motor coordination, and visual alertness. Because all three of these tasks require a high degree of concentration for success, this provided some evidence that George was being hindered in the educational process by either constitutionally based attentional deficits or an underlying emotional component which was causing this inconsistency in attentional skills. Also to be considered in hypothesizing about his condition was the possibility of a specific learning disability in the areas of visual or auditory processing.

Further educational tests and tests of specific functioning were ordered as a result of the initial WISC–R findings. It was discovered that the child did have problems in auditory sequencing and expressed difficulties in letter and word recognition. A meeting with school authorities was recommended in order to design an individualized educational program for George. Educational interventions might include perceptual training, sensory integrative remediation, and help in improving motor coordination. Since his behavioral problems were also partly seen as a manifestation of family tensions, a recommendation to include his parents in the therapeutic process was made.

McCarthy Scales of Children's Abilities

The McCarthy Scales of Children's Abilities are individually administered tests of young children's intellectual functioning.[12] They were well standardized on children 2½ to 8½ years of age. For practical purposes, however, the McCarthy scales find their greatest usefulness in the assessment of children aged 3 to 6. With children younger than 3 years, it may be difficult to identify delays clearly. For children older than 6 years who may be having further evaluations in the future, a test such as the Wechsler Intelligence Scale for Children—Revised may have greater usefulness because of its ability to assess functioning up through age 16 years.

In addition to providing a general level of intellectual functioning, the McCarthy Scales provide the clinician with a profile of an individual child's functioning in the following areas: verbal ability, nonverbal reasoning ability, number aptitude, short-term memory, and fine-motor and gross-motor coordination. It is also possible to assess right–left hand dominance. When attempting to detect early evidence of possible learning disabilities it is extremely important to be able to assess with reliability these important components of intellectual ability.

The McCarthy Scales comprise 18 different tests which cluster into the five scales described above. There are five verbal tests, seven perceptual-performance tests, three quantitative tests, four memory tests, and five motor tests. Several of the tests fall in two of the five scales. For example, drawing a human figure is considered both a motor task and a perceptual-performance task.

The McCarthy Scales make use of highly attractive materials and most children find the procedures quite enjoyable. Tests are arranged in an order that is conducive to obtaining a youngster's optimum functioning. The development of rapport is facilitated by providing several nonverbal tasks before the youngster is asked to verbalize. These initial verbalizations are of a one-word nature which helps most youngsters overcome the anxiety involved in talking to strangers. Toward the middle of the examination process, the child has an opportunity to engage in gross motor tasks (balancing on one foot, skipping, etc.) which provides a break from the more tedious table work.

The examiner must be well qualified and familiar with the manual and testing materials. The 18 tests are administered one after the other, most starting at the basic level and then working up to a youngster's best functioning within that test. Testing generally stops on a particular test when the youngster has made several consecutive errors. The

administration rules permit the examiner to model successful performance on some of the perceptual-performance tasks, as well as to complete tasks that the youngster is unable to complete. These procedures
help minimize anxiety and frustration and add to the test's attractive-
ness for children.

All test items are scored according to standard procedures described
in the manual. At times, subtle judgments are required. For children
below the age of 5, approximately 45 to 50 minutes are required for the
total administration. Older children require approximately one hour.

When all the tests are administered, standard scores for the five
scales are calculated. Each scale has a mean of 50 and a standard deviation of 10. The General Cognitive Index score (GCI) is based on the sum
of the verbal scale score, the perceptual-performance scale score, and
the quantitative scale score. The GCI has a mean of 100 and a standard
deviation of 16. Although it is not called an IQ score, it is clear that
the GCI resembles an IQ, conceptually and statistically.[12] However, it
should be pointed out that in studies involving learning-disabled students, their GCI scores were generally lower than their IQ scores, on
the average of about 15 points. Additionally, some school systems continue to insist on "IQ" scores and may not accept the GCI.

In addition to the five scales noted above, researchers have found
that the various tests can be clustered into other areas of intellectual
functioning. Calculating age-equivalent scores in these areas permits
the examiner an opportunity to uncover learning weaknesses. One useful strategy involves comparing the youngster's performance in the
following areas: verbal-conceptualization abilities, visual-organizational
abilities, sequencing abilities, and acquired knowledge.[18]

A short form of the McCarthy Scales has been developed for use
as a screening instrument for preschool readiness.[19] Below-average scores
on the short form indicate a need for a more thorough evaluation with
the entire test.

The standardization sample included more than 100 children for
each of 10 age levels. The reliability of the McCarthy Scales is satisfactory
as is its concurrent validity with the Stanford-Binet, WISC–R, and WPPSI.
Factor analytic techniques reveal good construct validity. Again, as
noted above, children with learning disabilities tend to score lower on
the McCarthy Scales compared to the Stanford-Binet or WISC–R.

Because there is no clear evidence that the educational remediation should be directed toward specific weaknesses noted in a child's
performance on the McCarthy Scales, its use may be more appropriate
in classification than in programming.[13]

CASE ILLUSTRATION

Andy J., a 5½-year-old boy, was referred for evaluation by his pediatrician because of inappropriate behavior at school. Andy is Panamanian and has been in his current adoptive home since the age of 2½. He has lived in this area for approximately one year and as a result has had only limited experiences in hearing and speaking English.

The McCarthy Scales of Children's Abilities was included in the test battery. He achieved the following scores:

Verbal Index Scale	40
Perceptual-Performance Scale	58
Quantitative Index Score	42
General Cognitive Index	87
Memory Scale Index	39
Motor Scale Index	56

Andy's present intellectual functioning falls at the upper end of the low average range. On verbal tests and on perceptual-performance tests containing complicated verbal directions, Andy performed with some difficulty. Therefore his performance on this instrument was probably influenced by his limited experience with English. Analysis of his particular strengths and weaknesses indicates that considerable variability exists among Andy's intellectual abilities. Although his weaknesses on the verbal scale may reflect his limited experience with English, his strong scores on the perceptual-performance subtests indicate generally sound visual-spatial organizational abilities as well as sound nonverbal reasoning skills.

Some of this youngster's classroom difficulties may be a function of his difficulties in receptive and expressive language, and further assessment of language processing should be performed. For additional clarification, assessment with a Spanish language version of an intelligence test was recommended, as was follow-up testing with the McCarthy Scales as soon as Andy becomes more familiar with English.

Kaufman Assessment Battery for Children

The Kaufman Assessment Battery for Children (K–ABC) is a new and innovative measure of intelligence and achievement in children ages 2½ to 12½.[3] This test battery employs a strong theoretical base, rigorously developed, selected test items, and sophisticated standardization methodologies. The result is a test that not only understands and measures childhood intelligence in a way that differs from other tests but also measures achievement separately and facilitates educational planning.

The K–ABC relies on a conception of intelligence that is based on theory and research in neuropsychology and cognitive psychology. Rather than stressing the content of intelligence (as does, e.g., the WISC–R in its Verbal and Performance Scales), the K–ABC emphasizes the mental processes involved in problem solving by distinguishing between sequential and simultaneous processing. Sequential processing, regardless of verbal or nonverbal content, involves the arranging of input in serial order, with each part related to the preceding part in a linear or temporal way. Stimuli are thus processed feature by feature. The K–ABC has three sequential subtests, each with a mean of 10 and a standard deviation of 3. In school-related activities, sequential processing relates to the stepwise procedures used in "borrowing," following multistep commands, learning rules of grammar, and so forth.

Simultaneous processing involves spatial, analogical, or organizational tasks that, to be solved successfully, require simultaneous integration and synthesis (see Figure 9). Many stimuli are processed at once to produce gestalt or holistic impressions. The K–ABC has five subtests with simultaneous processing demands, each with a mean of 10 and

Figure 9. A sample of a Gestalt Closure item similar to those on the Simultaneous Processing Scale of the K–ABC. The child would be asked to identify this common item (bicycle) using the available cues. (Copyright 1983 by Alan S. Kaufman and Nadeen L. Kaufman, American Guidance Service and used by permission.)

standard deviation of 3. Academically, simultaneous processing is involved in tasks such as learning the shapes of numbers and letters, understanding themes in stories, and acquiring complex mathematical principles. The K–ABC assesses these two mental processes through a total of ten subtests (although not all are administered at each age level).

Overall intelligence is derived by combining the Sequential and Simultaneous Scales' standard scores into a Mental Processing Composite (a standard score with a mean of 100 and standard deviation of 15). Combining these two scores is theoretically supported because of Kaufman's notion that intelligence is complex and requires an integration of both sequential and simultaneous processing.[3]

In addition to the mental processing portions of the K–ABC there is an Achievement Scale which comprises a distinct set of six subtests that assess a youngster's fund of factual information and acquired academic information. Various subtests measure reading, arithmetic, general information, early language development, and language concepts. These individual achievement subtests combine into a global Achievement Scale with a mean of 100 and a standard deviation of 15. Its major purpose is to estimate a youngster's current and future academic accomplishments. Disparities among the Achievement Scale's subtest scores and differences between the Mental Processing Composite and Achievement Scale can be used to diagnose learning disabilities.

A special feature of the K–ABC is its ability to estimate, with a special combination of subtests, intellectual potential in children aged 4½ years to 12½ years who have communication problems. The total score of these "nonverbal" subtests correlates well with the total score of the entire test. The subtests included in this nonverbal scale vary from one age group to another. In all cases the directions can be spoken or acted out in pantomime. The nonverbal scale, like the Composite Scale, has a mean set at 100 and standard deviation at 15.

The test's authors stress the usefulness of the K–ABC with virtually all exceptional children including learning-disabled, behaviorally disordered, mentally retarded, hearing-impaired, physically handicapped, and gifted. The test is individually administered by a psychologist familiar with the procedures, materials, and interpretation process. Administration requires 30 to 50 minutes for preschoolers and 50 to 80 minutes for older children. The materials have been designed to maximize the child's interest and motivation. Administration procedures allow for the examiner to teach the proper problem-solving "set" which minimizes frustrations and anxieties for the children. Scoring rules have been devised to minimize examiners' subjectivity and maximize interrater reliability.

The actual interpretation of scores involves a multistage process. The test authors encourage the use of "bands of error" in describing an individual's score in order to reduce the opportunity of overinterpretation of any particular score. For example, a youngster obtaining a Mental Processing Composite score of 83 would be described as scoring in the 77 to 89 range (with 90% confidence). To further effective understanding and communication of test results, examiners are encouraged also to make use of descriptive categories for global scores (viz., lower extreme, well below average, below average, average, above average, well above average, and upper extreme) and to compare a youngster's scores with national, racial and sociocultural norms.

Further analyses of test results involve comparing standard scores for the Sequential and Simultaneous Processing Scales and then comparing Mental Processing and Achievement Scales standard scores. Next, the examiner notes strengths and weaknesses among the Mental Processing subtests and Achievement subtests. Well-developed and thorough statistical materials are included in the test manuals to facilitate this comparative process. The examiner then generates hypotheses to explain any significant variability among subtests based on the particular patterns of strengths and weaknesses (e.g., verbal processing weaknesses, sequential processing difficulties and so on).

The final interpretive step is translating the test results into meaningful educational implications and recommendations. The test authors stress that these recommendations comprise the most important outcome of the evaluation. As noted earlier, the sequential-simultaneous model used by the K–ABC has considerable applicability to classroom teaching. Recent research has provided impressive findings regarding how effective remediation (at least in reading skills) can be accomplished by teaching a youngster through his or her mental processing strength.[20]

Correlations between the K–ABC's Mental Processing Composite and other more traditional measures of intelligence (e.g., IQ scores) provide evidence for acceptable validity. At the same time, psychometric analyses support the claim that the K–ABC is more than a mere duplication of already existing measures in that it adds additional information about a child's cognitive functioning.

Because the K–ABC is so new and different, actual clinical impressions regarding its usefulness will have to wait the passing of time. Clinicians will need time to learn the administration, scoring, and interpretive complexities of the K–ABC and to see when and where in the total assessment battery the K–ABC should be used. However, because of the instrument's strong theoretical base, thorough standardization and normative referencing, and clear implications for educational remediation, it may become an important contribution to the clinical assessment of children.

CASE ILLUSTRATION (adapted from the K–ABC Manual)

Larry Z. is a 4½-year-old boy referred for an evaluation by his mother and preschool teacher because of behavior problems, including "not listening" and inappropriate, aggressive interactions with schoolmates. During an observation period prior to formal testing, Larry was noted to play with considerable focus and goal directedness. He was more comfortable using gestures than words to communicate his needs. On the K–ABC he obtained the following scores:

Global Scale	Standard Score
Sequential Processing	74
Simultaneous Processing	103
Mental Processing Composite	88
Achievement	88

Achievement	Score
Expressive Vocabulary	102
Faces and Places	109
Arithmetic	74
Riddles	75

MENTAL PROCESSING SCALED SCORES

Sequential Processing	Score
Hand Movements	9
Number Recall	2
Word Order	6

Simultaneous Processing	Score
Magic Windows	12
Face Recognition	7
Gestalt Closure	15
Triangles	8

Larry's scores show a statistically significant difference between Sequential and Simultaneous Processing with clearcut superiority in processing material in a holistic manner, being able to deal with several features of a stimulus at once. His variability among achievement subtest scores (two clear-cut strengths and two clear-cut weaknesses) reflects poor auditory comprehension. His strong Simultaneous Processing score supports this interpretation and provides evidence of average processing in the visual modality. It

*was recommended that more specific tests of psycholinguistic func-
tioning be administered. Results of that testing confirmed that Larry's auditory comprehension difficulties were contributing to his
behavior problems. Referrals were made to a language therapist
and mental health professional.*

Leiter International Performance Scale

The Leiter International Performance Scale[2] is a nonverbal measure of intelligence for individuals 3 years to 18 years of age. It originally
appeared in 1940, following 13 years of preparatory work involving
ethnic groups in the Hawaiian Islands. It was revised in 1948, after its
application in the testing of American children of Army recruits during
the Second World War. The Leiter is most useful in estimating intellectual functioning in individuals who, for a variety of reasons, cannot
be evaluated with more conventional intellectual measures. With
younger children, especially, the language demands of the Stanford-
Binet and Wechsler Scales may depress the scores obtained. When there
is a question about hearing and/or language deficits in these or other
youngsters, it is important to supplement the previously obtained measures of intelligence with scores obtained from a nonverbal measure of
intellectual functioning, such as the Leiter.

The Leiter continues to have some use as a culture-fair measure
of intellectual functioning, but its major use is in the assessment of
individuals with hearing, speech, or other types of language handicaps.
It can also be used in the assessment of individuals with motor
impairments.[21]

The Leiter makes use of the concept of mental age, and its construction resembles that of the Stanford-Binet Intelligence Scale. The
scale consists of 54 standardized tests which involve activities such as
color matching, analogies, series completion, visual discrimination, and
block construction. Six tests comprise each of the age groupings, which
appear at yearly intervals from ages 2 years through 18 years. As the
testing proceeds, the examiner establishes a basal level, which is the
latest age grouping at which all of the tests are passed, and proceeds
up through a ceiling level, which is the first age grouping at which all
of the tests are failed. In its standard administration, it is recommended
that two consecutive ceiling levels be reached before the testing is
completed.

The Leiter's materials consist of a slotted wooden frame that accepts
a different cardboard template for each of the various tests. Each test

consists of a number of wooden blocks that can be arranged to fit into the frame to complete a theme or solve a problem based on the cardboard template (see Figure 10).

Because the Leiter's major use is with individuals who have hearing and/or speech handicaps, the standardized administration procedures make use of nonverbal instructions. In most instances, the examiner either points to the materials in a prescribed fashion or completes a portion of the subtest to demonstrate the subtest's problem-solving strategy. All individuals are started at a level considerably below their chronological age to give them a chance to understand the general problem-solving expectations of the Scale. Administration time is approximately 30 to 45 minutes.

As in the Stanford-Binet, an individual's score is based on the number of months' credit earned. For example, an individual with a basal score at the 4-year level, with two tests passed at the 5-year and 6-year levels and no tests passed at the 7-year and 8-year levels, would earn a mental age of 4 years, 4 months. This mental age score is used to calculate an IQ score based on the individual's chronological age. The examiner must be familiar with some calculation peculiarities of this particular test instrument to arrive at the IQ score.

The Leiter's IQ score tends to correlate quite strongly with other accepted measures of intellectual functioning.[7] Some caution must be

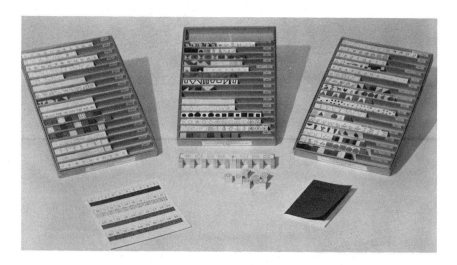

Figure 10. The test apparatus for the Leiter International Performance Test. (Photo courtesy of Stoelting Co., Chicago.)

exercised, however, in generalizing this score when obtained by individuals with hearing and/or language handicaps. The developmental experiences of these individuals may influence their intellectual functioning, and it may be misleading to speculate about a hearing-impaired individual's general intellectual functioning using a score based on norms generated with a hearing population. Also, although the various Leiter tests sample a variety of intellectual skills, the actual skills sampled may not resemble completely the intellectual skills sampled by other more traditional intellectual measures.

The Leiter has been criticized because of a number of limitations,[7] the most serious of which are its psychometric problems (outdated norms and inadequate standardization). Nevertheless, it continues to have considerable usefulness in testing handicapped children who cannot be tested with more traditional intelligence tests.[21,7]

CASE ILLUSTRATION

Joel T., 5 years, 9 months old, was referred for evaluation by his kindergarten teacher because of insufficient progress in his preacademic skill development. Compared to other youngsters in the class, Joel was described as not "listening" and falling behind in basic skills; he was also a constant behavior problem. During psychological testing, Joel was attentive but easily frustrated. On the Stanford-Binet, he achieved a mental age of 4 years, 3 months and an IQ score of 65. Because of his confusion on some of the tasks requiring verbal processing and relative ease on perceptual-motor tasks, it was decided to administer the Leiter International Performance Scale. On this nonverbal test of intellectual functioning, Joel was able to pass all of the subtests at the 4-year level, three of the six subtests at the 5-year level, and two of the subtests at the 6-year level. He failed all subtests at the 7 and 8-year levels. The result was a mental age of 4 years, 5 months and an IQ score of 82. The disparity between his scores on the verbally bound Stanford-Binet and nonverbal Leiter International Performance Scale pointed out this youngster's difficulties with verbal processing. A thorough speech, hearing, and language assessment was recommended.

References

1. Anastasi A: *Psychological Testing*, ed 4. New York, Macmillan, 1976.
2. Leiter RG: *Leiter International Performance Scale*. Chicago, Stoelting, 1948.
3. Kaufman AS, Kaufman NL: *Interpretive Manual for the Kaufman Assessment Battery for Children*. Circle Pines, MI, American Guidance Service, 1983.

4. Buros OK: *The Eighth Mental Measurement Yearbook.* Highland Park, NJ, Gryphon Press, 1978.
5. Bayley N: *Bayley Scales of Infant Development: Birth to Two Years.* New York, Psychological Corporation, 1969.
6. Cattell P: *Cattell Infant Intelligence Scale.* New York, Psychological Corporation, 1940.
7. Sattler JM: *Assessment of Children's Intelligence and Special Abilities,* ed 2. Boston, Allyn and Bacon, 1982, p 254.
8. Collard RR: Review of the Preschool Attainment Record, research edition. In Buros OK (ed): *Seventh Mental Measurement Yearbook.* Highland Park, NJ, Gryphon Press, 1972, p 759–760.
9. Terman LM, Merill MA: *Stanford-Binet Intelligence Scale.* Boston, Houghton Mifflin, 1960.
10. Hagen E, Sattler JM, Thorndike RL: *Stanford-Binet Intelligence Scale,* ed 4. Chicago, Riverside Publishing Company, 1985.
11. Wechsler D: *Manual for the Wechsler Intelligence Scale for Children—Revised.* New York, Psychological Corporation, 1974.
12. McCarthy DA: *Manual for the McCarthy Scales of Children's Abilities.* New York, Psychological Corporation, 1972.
13. Helton GB, Workman EA, Matuszek PA: *Psychoeducational Assessment: Integrating Concepts and Techniques.* New York, Grune & Stratton, 1982, p 139.
14. Wechsler D: *Manual for the Wechsler Preschool and Primary Scale of Intelligence.* New York, Psychological Corporation, 1967.
15. Wechsler D: *Manual for the Weschsler Adult Intelligence Scale—Revised.* New York, Psychological Corporation, 1981.
16. Wechsler D: *Wechsler Intelligence Scale for Children.* New York, Psychological Corporation, 1949.
17. Kaufman AS: *Intelligence Testing with the WISC–R.* New York, Wiley-Interscience, 1979.
18. Kaufman AS, Kaufman NL: *Clinical Evaluation of Young Children with the McCarthy Scales.* New York, Grune & Stratton, 1977.
19. Kaufman AS: A McCarthy Shortform for rapid screening of preschool, kindergarten, and first-grade children. *Contemporary Educational Psychology* 2:149–257, 1977.
20. Gunnison JA, Kaufman NL, Kaufman AS: Sequential and simultaneous processing applied to remediation. *Academic Therapy* 17:297–307, 1982.
21. Wright L, Schaefer AB, Solomons G: *Encyclopedia of Pediatric Psychology.* Baltimore, University Park Press, 1979.

Chapter 8

Educational and Perceptual Testing

When school-aged children are referred to the clinician for diagnosis, it is helpful to assess educational achievement since often academic problems are associated with a broad range of behavioral dysfunction.[1] Assessing performance in school subject areas is also important in monitoring a child's learning progress as well as in preparing school programs or interventions. Achievement tests attempt to measure the effects of a relatively standardized set of academic experiences such as that obtained in the public school system. This is in contrast to readiness tests, for example, the Metropolitan Readiness Tests, which try to predict how well prepared a child might be for school.[2]

It is common practice for the psychologist to include individually administered tests of achievement within his or her test battery. These tests are usually constituted to measure performance in a variety of school subjects. The resulting scores are typically presented on the basis of school grade equivalents. For instance, a child's score of 3.5 on a spelling achievement test suggests that his or her spelling level is similar to that of an average child in the middle of the third grade. Two of the most widely used individually administered achievement tests, the Wide Range Achievement Test (WRAT) and the Peabody Individual Achievement Test (PIAT) will be discussed in this chapter.

Occasionally, psychologists are requested to assess specific functioning in a child when a handicapping condition or a specific learning disability might be present which impedes learning. One such test, the

Illinois Test of Psycholinguistic Abilities, is also reviewed in this chapter. This instrument attempts to delineate deficient areas of a child's language functioning. It was developed to help in planning for remedial work in this extremely important area of development.

It is also important to measure other types of abilities such as visual perception and visual-motor integration. The Bender Visual Motor Gestalt Test and the Developmental Test of Visual Motor Integration, both described in this section, are examples of tests of perceptual motor maturation. Through the years these types of tests have also been used by clinicians and educators to detect signs of organicity or emotional difficulties.

Illinois Test of Psycholinguistic Abilities

The Illinois Test of Psycholinguistic Abilities (ITPA) is an individually administered measure designed to assess a child's ability to comprehend, process, and relate both verbal and nonverbal material.[3] It is used with children between the ages of 2 years, 4 months and 10 years, 3 months. The test is based on the theoretical foundation of Osgood's psycholinguistic communication model.[4]

The ITPA is composed of ten standard and two supplementary subtests. Each of the subtests is constructed so as to reduce the demands of any factor other than what is being assessed.[5] For instance, the subtests which purport to measure comprehension (auditory and visual reception) reduce the number of alternative responses for the child by simplifying the answers to either yes or no or pointing responses.

The ITPA is divided into two levels of organization. One, the representational level, focuses on language symbols. Subtests in this section include measures of auditory and visual reception and association, and manual and verbal expression. The other, the automatic level, concentrates on those aspects of linguistic ability which are well organized and habitual. The subtests in this section include closure (auditory, visual, and grammatical), sound blending, and sequential memory (both auditory and visual).

A list of the subtests of the ITPA with the types of abilities being measured follows.

1. *Auditory Reception.* This subtest measures the ability to understand the spoken word through a series of yes–no questions.

2. *Visual Reception.* This is a multiple-choice subtest assessing memory for visually presented pictures which are related.
3. *Auditory Association.* This is a verbal analogies subtest requiring the child to relate concepts presented orally.
4. *Visual Association.* This is a visual analogies subtest in which the stimuli are visual, the directions oral, and the child points to the answer.
5. *Verbal Expression.* This subtest requires the child to describe orally objects which are familiar.
6. *Manual Expression.* This subtest measures the child's knowledge in understanding how to use various objects.
7. *Grammatical Closure.* In this subtest, the child must use the correct grammatical forms of a word to complete a statement.
8. *Auditory Closure.* This is a supplementary subtest requiring the child to complete words with one or more syllables missing.
9. *Sound Blending.* This is a supplementary subtest requiring the child to synthesize words when only fragments are presented orally.
10. *Visual Closure.* This subtest requires recognizing familiar objects from an incomplete visual presentation.
11. *Auditory Sequential Memory.* This is a digit subtest in which reproduction of orally presented numbers is required in proper sequence.
12. *Visual Sequential Memory.* This subtest measures the ability to reproduce meaningless designs from memory.

By analyzing a child's performance on these twelve subtests, the clinician can sketch a profile and make inferences for remedial interventions. A psycholinguistic age score (PLA), which is an overall index of the level of psycholinguistic development of the child, can also be calculated. Finally, a psycholinguistic quotient (PLQ), which is a ratio score, can be obtained by dividing the PLQ by the child's chronological age and multiplying by 100. The PLQ describes the general rate, not level, of psycholinguistic development.[6] An estimate of the child's mental age can also be derived by using the original normative group as a basis for conversion.

The ITPA was standardized on a sample of children consisting of 962 boys and girls of average intelligence and middle-class backgrounds. No children were used who were displaying difficulties in school, although the test purportedly was designed "for use with children encountering learning difficulties."[7] Preschoolers were selected by testing younger siblings of the school sample and by referrals from mothers of these children. Information regarding the intelligence of the normative sample also attests to the fact that this group of children was extremely narrowly defined.[5]

The ITPA has been criticized because of these limitations in the collection of normative data.[8] It has also been criticized for its use of incorrect reliability techniques, its emphasis on middle-class speech patterns, and its limited value in making educational distinctions because of a lack of evidence that it actually assesses ten different areas of functioning.[8] Some clinicians consider the ITPA to be nothing more than an additional test of individual intelligence.

The primary advantage of the ITPA appears to be in its ability to delineate areas that require remedial work.[6] The differentiation of various aspects of linguistic functioning into a model of comprehension (decoding) and production (encoding) and offering a distinction between input and output channels involved in the communication process also seems to be potentially favorable. However, a major limitation of the test is its nearly total concentration on language functions.[6]

Peabody Individual Achievement Test

The Peabody Individual Achievement Test (PIAT) is a norm-referenced, individually administered screening device intended to provide a multifaceted overview in five salient areas of academic achievement—mathematics, reading recognition, reading comprehension, spelling, and general information.[9] It is used with children from kindergarten through high school and typically takes between 30 to 40 minutes to administer. Four types of scores are derived from each of the five subtests and a fifth score is obtained for the overall results. These scores include age and grade equivalents, percentile ranks, and standard scores which are based on a distribution mean of 100 and a standard deviation of 15.

The following achievement behaviors are sampled by the PIAT subtests:

1. *Mathematics.* This is a subtest of 84 multiple-choice problems ranging from such basic skills as matching, discriminating, and recognizing numerals to measuring relations in geometry and

trigonometry. The problems are devised with emphasis on applying mathematical knowledge to solutions.

2. *Reading Recognition.* This set of 84 questions is an oral reading subtest with difficulty levels ranging from preschool through high school. It measures ability development in matching and naming letters and in reading aloud individual words. It assesses skills in translating alphabetic symbols into comprehensible speech sounds.

3. *Reading Comprehension.* A 66-item subtest in a multiple choice format. Sentences of increasing difficulty are read; then the child must demonstrate understanding by selecting the correct answer from a group of four pictures. This subtest assesses the child's ability to obtain meaning from printed words.

4. *Spelling.* This 84-item subtest samples the child's ability to identify letters from four words the accurate spelling of which is read aloud by the examiner. Beginning items measure the child's skill in recognizing a printed letter from pictured objects and to relate letter symbols with speech sounds.

5. *General Information.* Consisting of 84 orally presented questions which the child answers verbally, this test assesses the amount of learned knowledge the child has acquired in fine arts, sports, science, and social studies. This subtest, like "Information" on the Wechsler Scales, assesses how the child has assimilated the surrounding culture.

All items in each of the subtests are introduced in ascending difficulty. Completion of all items is not anticipated as only those items within a critical range are administered. This range consists of a basal level defined as five consecutive correct answers to a ceiling level at which five errors within any seven consecutive responses are made. Therefore the examiner could assume that the administered problems will be appropriate and challenging to the child, regardless of age or level of ability.

Test materials used in the PIAT are included in two volumes of spiral-bound kits. Each volume presents the questions to the child at eye level with the examiner's directions on the back side. The test plates contain demonstration and training exercises as well as the actual test items. The exercises, a unique feature of the PIAT, are used as a structured preparation package to aid young and immature children in test requirements. They are repeated until the child answers all items in a set accurately in proper sequence, or until three minutes have elapsed. Once these exercises have been successfully completed few children will find the test items uncomprehensible and will pass at least one or possibly two of the questions.[9] This special feature, combined with the knowledge that only simple responses (e.g., pointing) are required from the majority of the subtest, makes the materials especially relevant to children of low abilities.

The standardization sample for the PIAT consisted of 2,889 public day school children of both sexes who were attending regular classes. Twenty-nine school districts involving nine geographical regions took part in the development process with at least 200 children at each grade level represented. Although this standardization appears superior to other similar tests of achievement, the reliabilities of the subtests have been considered too low for use in making important educational decisions.[5] The PIAT appears to serve as a test to locate broad levels of achievement, after which a more comprehensive test (e.g., Woodcock-Johnson Psycho-Educational Battery[10]) is required.[11] Therefore teachers must judge its appropriateness for their particular curricula.

CASE ILLUSTRATION

James P., 11 years, 4 months old, was a product of multiple home placements. James lived with his parents until age 5, then was shifted to his grandparents until age 8 due to familial disharmony. After that, he was placed in several group homes where his difficult behavior caused him either to run away or become aggressive.

James' early development was also characterized by many problems. He was seen at local hospitals for malnutrition at ages 3 and 4. He had a history of fire setting, once at age 5, then later while at a group home. His school history, also described as volatile, was noteworthy for physical aggressiveness, temper tantrums, and destructiveness of his own classwork. He repeated the third grade and was in a class for socially and emotionally disturbed at the time of this testing.

As part of a comprehensive psychological battery requested from the group home, James was given the PIAT to provide an overview of his academic achievement. Results from an IQ test (WISC–R) suggested low average functioning with Performance skills markedly superior to Verbal abilities.

James obtained the following scores on the PIAT:

	Raw score	Grade equivalent	Percentile rank	Standard score
Mathematics	*37*	*3.5*	*9*	*80*
Reading Recognition	*30*	*3.1*	*6*	*77*
Reading Comprehension	*27*	*2.6*	*3*	*71*

Spelling	32	3.2	4	74
General Information	28	3.8	12	82
Total Test	154	3.1	7	78

According to these results, James's level of academic readiness was comparable to an average child entering the third grade. This placed him approximately two years behind the expected grade level for his chronological age in most areas of achievement. Because of his history of emotional upheaval and limited verbal functioning, placement in the special class appeared appropriate. Additional testing was recommended to specify specific weaknesses and plan appropriate interventions.

Wide Range Achievement Test

The Wide Range Achievement Test (WRAT) provides an estimate of an individual's academic achievement.[12] The WRAT has had four revisions since its original publication in 1936. The latest revision was in 1978 and utilized more sophisticated scaling techniques than the earlier editions, although the items in the latest three editions are identical. The WRAT assesses the acquisition of basic skills in reading, spelling, and arithmetic. The reading test requires the child to recognize and name letters and to pronounce words (word attack skills). The spelling test requires the child to copy letter-like marks, print his or her name, and write dictated words. The arithmetic test includes counting, recognition of numbers, and computation. Within the three areas, items are arranged in terms of increasing difficulty.

The WRAT is an individually administered test. The examiner should be familiar with general testing considerations, specific test procedures, and scoring and interpretation procedures. Two distinct sets of items comprise the WRAT: Level I for ages 5 years, 0 months to 11 years, 11 months; Level II for ages 12 years to adult. Administration time is approximately 20 to 30 minutes. Specific test items are scored objectively as right or wrong. Raw scores for each area are converted to grade equivalents, standard scores, and percentiles. It should be noted that the standard score (with a mean of 100 and a standard deviation of 15) is the more accurate and therefore the preferred one to use, as the grade ratings tend to be inflated and/or otherwise inaccurate for many groups. The standard score can be used in comparison to a child's performance on other measures, typically intellectual functioning. Significant differences between a child's abilities (e.g., as reflected in IQ score) and achievements (e.g., WRAT standard scores) can be a reflection of a learning disability.

Measures of reliability and validity for the WRAT are acceptable.[12] When correlated with traditional intellectual tests WRAT scores are more strongly associated with verbal measures of intelligence than with performance measures. The WRAT's various revisions tend to produce somewhat inconsistent standard scores and grade ratings.[8] That is, an individual's functioning across time can be best understood using the same version of this test.

Criticisms of the WRAT include its limited item content (e.g., no evaluation of reading comprehension) which makes generalization of broader academic skills difficult.[13] Consequently, its usefulness in educational diagnostics is limited.[13]

The WRAT's greatest utility comes in situations in which academic screening is needed, for example, in the context of a general psychological test battery. When the standard scores on the WRAT differ significantly from the full scale IQ score on a general test of intelligence such as the WISC–R or when there is significant variability among the three WRAT standard scores, referral for more thorough psychoeducational testing is needed.[8] Unlike the WRAT, such testing can help to substantiate or rule out learning disabilities and can provide guidelines for specific educational programming.

CASE ILLUSTRATION

Charles B. is 10 years, 6 months old, a fifth-grader referred for a comprehensive psychological evaluation because of long-standing academic difficulties along with more recently developed behavior problems. During testing Charles proved to be a shy, slow-to-warm youngster, hesitant to provide much in the way of verbal responses. He was more interested in manipulative and paper–pencil tasks.

His Full Scale WISC–R IQ was 95 but a statistically significant difference was found between his Verbal IQ (88) and his Performance IQ (105). That this discrepancy might be a product of a learning disability was supported by his pattern of scores on the WRAT:

	Grade rating	Standard score	Percentile
Reading	3.0	79	8
Spelling	3.3	81	10
Arithmetic	4.9	98	45

These scores reflect lags in Charles's acquisition of basic phonetic and word attack skills but adequate arithmetic skills. These levels of achievement are not commensurate with what would be expected from a youngster of his intelligence. To substantiate the presence of a language-processing weakness, further psycholin-guistic and psychoeducational evaluations were recommended. Eventual provision of learning disability resource programming helped to improve Charles's academic functioning, and a decline in his behavior problems was also achieved.

Bender Visual Motor Gestalt Test

The Bender Visual Motor Gestalt Test, commonly referred to as the Bender, was originally constructed as a visual-motor performance task with adult clinical patients and as a developmental screening examination for children.[14] The nine geometrical designs used in the Bender were based on the work of Max Wertheimer, one of the origi-nators of the Gestalt school of psychology. The designs (as shown in Figure 11) consist of dots, lines, angles, and curves which form a variety of relationships. Each design is on a card which approximates the size of an enlarged index card.

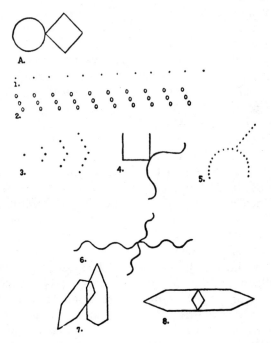

Figure 11. From the Bender Visual Motor Gestalt Test. (Copyright 1938 by the American Orthopsychiatric Association and used by permission.)

The underlying principle in the use of these designs, as expounded by the Gestalt school, was that the organized whole (i.e., structured units) is the primary form of perception in humans. Any loss or distortion of this integrative perception might therefore allude to expressions of pathology. It was believed that neural insults, emotional problems, or variations in intellectual functioning could possibly impact on this total process of perception and reproduction. These possibilities of distorting influence were originally explored by Lauretta Bender, a child psychiatrist, with people suffering from aphasia, organic brain syndrome, schizophrenia, manic-depression, mental retardation, and severe anxiety, along with normal children.[14]

The Bender requires both perceptual-motor focus and discrimination.[15] At a basic level, the child must have the ability to concentrate and pay attention to the figure, while at a more complex level, the child must be able to separate the design and then integrate it into a unified whole or *Gestalt*. For example, a child may be able to differentiate a design as consisting of two parts but not be able to reproduce the parts (e.g., drawing two circles instead of a square and a circle as in Design A). Motor behavior also incorporates both of these abilities.

Furthermore, a developmental milestone for every child is the ability to focus on one movement and to discriminate between movements. In order to complete the Bender designs, a child must have reached a level of maturity that allows him or her to hold a drawing utensil without opposing movements which would impede performance. It is also important for the child to choose appropriate movements which allow him or her to make accurate drawings.

Age thus becomes an important factor in the use of the Bender. For example, as a developmental indicator, the Bender should be used only during a particular maturational period. Children whose developmental level is below 6 years of age are likely to do so poorly that interpretations would be inappropriate. Reasonably valid mental ages can be obtained when using the Bender with children up to age 12. Moreover, indicators for brain damage from protocols of children's responses are quite disparate from adult drawings, especially from children under 10 years of age.

Since its inception, the Bender has become extensively used throughout the world in both clinics and hospitals as a screening device and as a portion of the psychological test battery to aid in the assessment of developmental, cognitive-perceptual, and emotional problems during evaluations of children and adults. It has been found to be useful in: (1) establishing rapport with the child, (2) assessing uneducated or culturally deprived individuals, (3) detailing areas of emotional conflict, (4) predicting certain segments of school achievement, (5) studying intercultural differences, (6) investigating the connection between perceptual-motor behavior and various personality traits, (7) estimating intelligence, (8) identifying juvenile delinquents, and (9) discovering learning disturbances (adapted from Hutt[16]).

It would hardly be accurate to address the Bender as if it were a single instrument. There are many versions of the test with varying methods of administration, scoring, and interpretation.[17] This brief outline will attempt to address the salient aspects of administering the designs and discuss the more popular scoring methods.

The child is usually presented with a stack of papers nearby on an examining table with pencils and eraser. He or she is then instructed to copy the series of simple figures as well as possible. Typically, one sheet of paper is placed in front of the child, although some examiners prefer the child to select the paper from the stack so as to provide minimal guidance. After the presentation of the initial card, the child often begins to inquire about direction, which may continue throughout the test. It has been deemed essential that the examiner place the burden of problem solving back on the child. All that is usually necessary in response to questions from an uncertain or inquisitive child is a statement of encouragement (e.g., "Do as well as you can").

The salient characteristic of this administration procedure is to allow the child an opportunity to adapt to the task in his or her personal, unique manner. The child's approach through use of spacing, size, and quality of reproductions and sequential placements are believed to be expressions of the child's developmental capabilities, needs, and conflicts.[16]

Although many clinicians have attempted to construct suitable scoring methods, none has achieved universal acceptance. Throughout its earlier history, the simple inspection system, as developed by Bender,[14] was used as the main approach for analyzing the drawings. Hutt[16] later elaborated on this procedure to emphasize the projective aspects of the test performance. However, both systems met with much criticism because of vague normative values.

More recently Koppitz[18] provided a more precise scoring method based on norms collected from children ages five to ten. Her pioneering research included comparisons of scores obtained from these Bender protocols with intellectual functioning and academic success. In one study, she found that seven errors in copying figures discriminated between good and poor students of early elementary school age. These errors included distortion of shape, rotations, substitutions of circles or dashes for dots, perseveration, parts of figures not joined, three or more angles in a curve, and missing or extra angles. Additionally, she established a list of 29 indicators of brain damage for the Bender but cautioned that several of these signs must be evident before a plausible diagnosis can be made.

In its current use, the Koppitz Developmental Bender Scoring System is divided into two sections—developmental age scoring and emotional indicators. As a system in assessing maturation, the developmental scores are used for evaluating visual-motor functioning. Scorable errors, 30 in all, have been grouped into four categories: shape distortion, rotation, integration difficulties, and perseveration. The total number of errors is compared to normative values which have been constructed for ages 5 years, 0 months to 11 years, 11 months.[19]

Perceptual-motor tasks, such as the Bender, have sometimes been so exclusively constructed and/or utilized as instruments for detecting brain damage or dysfunction that examiners often ignore other possible interferences of perceptual-motor functioning. Importantly, it cannot be assumed that brain damage is the sole cause of deficient performance. Moderating influences such as developmental delays, sensory deprivation, motor weakness, injuries, fatigue, illness, poor motivation, socialcultural deprivation, intellectual retardation, and emotional disturbances could all interfere with achievement.

CASE ILLUSTRATION

A referral for a psychological evaluation of Fred S., aged 6 years, 7 months, was precipitated by his pediatrician's concern in Fred's development. In a recent pediatric examination (the first one by this physician), it was discovered that Fred reversed letters, could not repeat five numbers, could not distinguish between right and left, could not make alternating movements, and was unable to write any letters legibly. Also, the pediatrician indicated that Fred was approximately 1½ years delayed on a Draw-A-Person test which he had administered. The main question at the time was whether Fred was delayed in all areas of functioning or whether he had specific problems which were impeding his growth and development.

As part of a broader psychological evaluation, Fred was administered the Bender to ascertain his perceptual maturation and to screen for possible signs of organicity. Figure 12 shows his attempts at reproducing the figures.

Results for Fred's Bender did produce some evidence of perceptual-motor dysfunction and/or possible organic factors

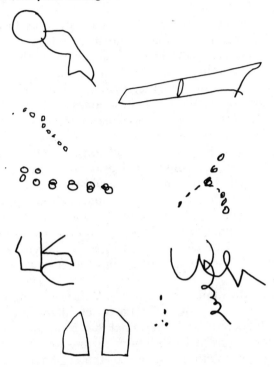

Figure 12. The Bender Visual Motor Gestalt Test of a boy 6 years, and 7 months old.

contribution to his scholastic problems. Based on the Koppitz Developmental Scoring System, 12 errors of shape distortion, rotation of figures, and integration (failure to complete or join figures) were noted. This number of errors for Fred is more than one standard deviation above the normal for his age and placed him in the 15th percentile of perceptual maturation with an age equivalent score of 5 years, 3 months.

Although Fred was not found to be delayed in all areas of functioning, the above problems as well as auditory sequencing deficits were discovered during the evaluation. Recommendations for additional medical and neurological evaluations, an audiological evaluation, and a program of educational remediation were suggested.

Developmental Test of Visual Motor Integration

The Developmental Test of Visual Motor Integration (VMI) is a design-copying test for children ages 2 to 15.[20] Like the Bender Gestalt test (see preceding section) and other instruments which require the reproduction of geometric figures, the VMI attempts to assess brain damage, visual memory, perceptual disturbance, and motor maturation.[21]

The VMI consists of 24 forms arranged in increasing difficulty which can be given either individually or in a group. The majority of the figures are straight-line/angular configurations, with 5 of the 24 having circular components. The instructions are clear and the test can be easily administered by a psychologist or classroom teacher in 15 minutes.

Scoring of the VMI is pass–fail and consists of counting the number of designs accurately constructed prior to a ceiling of three consecutive misses. The total number of successfully completed designs can then be converted into separate developmental-age equivalent norms for each sex. Scoring criteria are provided for each of the 24 designs with acceptable samples of actual reproductions given as an aid. Unfortunately, the scoring procedures tend to be vague with a high degree of subjectivity.[22] For instance, any doubt as to an acceptable response is scored correct.

The standardization sample for the VMI was composed of 1,039 children from Illinois. About one half of the children were from middle-class, suburban schools with the remainder from lower-middle-class urban and rural groups. All children were considered to be of average intelligence. According to one reviewer, the most adequate use of the VMI appears to be for ages 5 to 13, and then only for children from suburban schools.[22] There is no other specific information regarding the demographic characteristics of the standardization sample.

The VMI was constructed to detect children with school learning problems. As in other such tests of visual-motor integration, the sampling of task behavior is limited, although the 24 designs are a larger sample than the 9 figures on the Bender. Also, in relation to these other instruments, the VMI has comparatively high reliability. The validity of the device, however, is suspect. Its greatest asset is in relating results to chronological age. The expected developmental sequence involved in the accurate reproduction of geometric designs does hold some promise for the assessment of learning disabilities in the visual-motor area.

References

1. Erickson MT: Psychological assessment methods, in Gabel S, Erickson MT (eds): *Child Development and Developmental Disabilities.* Boston, Little, Brown, & Company, 1980, p 209.

2. Hildreth GH, Griffiths, NL: *Metropolitan Readiness Tests.* Tarrytown-on-Hudson, NY, World Book, 1949–1950.
3. Kirk SA, McCarthy, JJ, Kirk WD: *The Illinois Test of Psycholinguistic Abilities.* Urbana, University of Illinois Press, 1968.
4. Osgood CE: Motivational dynamics of language behavior, in Jones, MR (ed): *Nebraska Symposium on Motivation.* Lincoln, University of Nebraska Press, 1957, p 348.
5. Salvia J, Ysseldyke JE: *Assessment in Special and Remedial Education.* Boston, Houghton Mifflin Co, 1978.
6. Johnson SW, Morasky RL: *Learning Disabilities.* Boston, Allyn & Bacon Inc, p 107.
7. Paraskevopoulos JN, Kirk SA: *The Development and Psychometric Characteristics of the Revised Illinois Test of Psycholinguistic Abilities.* Urbana, University of Illinois Press, 1969.
8. Sattler JM: *Assessment of Children's Intelligence and Special Abilities,* ed 2. Boston, Allyn & Bacon Inc , 1982.
9. Dunn LC, Markwardt FC: *Peabody Individual Achievement Test Manual.* Circle Pines, MN, American Guidance Service, 1970.
10. Woodcock RW: *Woodcock-Johnson Psycho-Educational Battery: Technical Report.* Boston, Teaching Resources, 1977.
11. French JL: Review of the Peabody Individual Achievement Test, in Buros OK (ed): *The Seventh Mental Measurements Yearbook.* Highland Park, NJ, Gryphon Press, 1972, p 34.
12. Jastak JF, Jastak S: *The Wide Range Achievement Test (rev ed).* Wilmington, Del, Jastak Associates, 1978.
13. Helton GB, Workman EA, Matuszek PA: *Psychoeducational Assessment: Integrating Concepts and Techniques.* New York, Grune & Stratton, 1982.
14. Bender L: *A Visual Motor Gestalt Test and Its Clinical Use.* New York, American Orthopsychiatric Association, 1938.
15. Palmer JO: *The Psychological Assessment of Children.* New York, John Wiley & Sons Inc, 1970, p 212.
16. Hutt, M: *The Hutt Adaptation of the Bender-Gestalt Test,* ed 3. New York, Grune & Stratton Inc, 1963.
17. Golden CJ: *Clinical Interpretations of Objective Psychological Tests.* New York, Grune & Stratton Inc, 1979, p 132.
18. Koppitz E: *The Bender-Gestalt Test for Young Children.* New York, Grune & Stratton Inc, 1963.
19. Koppitz E: *The Bender-Gestalt Test for Young Children, Vol 2, Research and Application, 1963–1973.* New York, Grune & Stratton Inc, 1975.
20. Beery KE: *Developmental Test of Visual Motor Integration.* Chicago, Follett Educational Corporation, 1967.
21. Lenton DA: Review of the Developmental Test of Visual Motor Integration, in Buros OK (ed): *The Eighth Mental Measurements Yearbook.* Highland Park, NJ, Gryphon Press, 1978.
22. Chissom BS: Review of the Developmental Test of Visual Motor Integration, in Buros OK (ed): *The Seventh Mental Measurements Yearbook.* Highland Park, NJ, Gryphon Press, 1972.

Chapter 9

Neuropsychological Tests

Neuropsychological Test Batteries

Clinical neuropsychology is usually concerned with understanding the neuroanatomical correlates of behavior. Neuropsychological assessments are undertaken for a number of purposes including research, patient care, and diagnosis. Such testing may help to localize lesions, establish functional baseline data, establish prognosis, and assist in the planning of rehabilitation programs. Although there are a number of assessment tools useful for these purposes,[1] the Halstead-Reitan and Luria-Nebraska Batteries have become the most frequently used in the neuropsychological assessment of children.[2]

Although the neuropsychological assessment strategies underlying the Halstead-Reitan and Luria-Nebraska batteries differ, both are concerned with identifying the relationships that exist between the brain and behavior. The clinical use of these batteries has grown in use in recent years as interest in neuropsychological assessment of children has become stronger. Selz[3] identifies three reasons for this trend. One reason is the increasing acceptance of the fact that brain damage or dysfunction frequently underlies learning disabilities and emotional and behavioral disturbances. A second reason is the practical and legal need to sample a broader variety of abilities than is done by standard intelligence tests. Third, there is growing evidence that effective educational remediation requires identifying the child's particular pattern of processing strengths and weaknesses and then matching the pattern to teaching strategies.

For clinicians, it is important to distinguish between those patients who require referral to a neurologist and those who require referral to a clinical neuropsychologist. Generally, a neurological examination focuses on lower-level functions whereas a neuropsychological examination is more sensitive to higher-level cognitive processes.[4] More specifically, for problems involving acute changes from previous levels of behavioral or psychological functioning, referral must first be to a neurologist. Referral to a neuropsychologist is appropriate for problems of a more long-standing nature, including visual, auditory, or tactile processing difficulties; constructional apraxia (copying designs or free drawing); abstract reasoning or concept formation problems; receptive or expressive language deficits; and short-term or long-term memory problems. In actual practice, the primary health care provider typically makes the initial referral to the clinical psychologist who, after performing a basic battery of tests, confers with the original referring source as to whether more thorough neuropsychological testing will be helpful. In other clinical instances a neurologist and neuropsychologist may work together in assessing a particular problem and planning intervention strategies.

Since children's problems tend to be multifaceted, neuropsychological assessment can help sort out how neurological factors influence and interact with environmental and emotional factors. Neuropsychological assessment can be an important step in helping a youngster with brain damage or dysfunction and his or her family understand the problem objectively. Additionally, understanding a youngster's strengths and weaknesses can help teachers and parents to deal more effectively with particular children by utilizing areas of strength in setting educational and behavioral objectives.

Halstead-Reitan Neuropsychological Test Batteries for Children

The Halstead-Reitan Neuropsychological Test Batteries for children were developed by Ralph Reitan and were based on the work done in the 1930s and 1940s by W. C. Halstead[5] who, in 1935, established a neuropsychology laboratory at the University of Chicago to study brain–behavior relationships in patients with known brain lesions. Although neurologists had been interested in these issues for some time, Halstead's work served to crystallize and refine the assessment process. His initial battery consisted of those tests and procedures that best differentiated brain-damaged patients from the matched control group. Early validative research also made use of autopsy reports. Reitan added to the original battery other tests that were sensitive and valid for assessing the full range of abilities mediated by the brain and for detecting deficits in particular regions of the brain. The tests that were included in this battery were those that could be interpreted in a manner consistent with Reitan's view of neuropsychology inference.

For children ages 9 years to 14 years the Halstead Neuropsychological Test Battery for Children is used.[6] Children 5 years to 8 years are tested with the Reitan-Indiana Neuropsychological Test Battery for Children.[6] This battery was developed because many of the tasks on the older children's battery proved too difficult for younger children. For this younger child's battery Reitan simplified some tasks and provided others with downward extensions. In addition, he designed six tests specifically for this battery. Both of these batteries include the administration of the Wechsler Intelligence Scale for Children—Revised (see Chapter 7).

The Halstead Neuropsychological Test Battery for Children consists of the following measures:

The *Category Test* measures abstract reasoning and conceptual thinking. It consists of six sets of slides, each with a different conceptual principle determining the correct answer. The slides are rear-projected onto a milk-glass screen and the child is asked to depress one of four numbered levers corresponding to the correct answer. A correct choice produces the sound of a chime and an incorrect choice produces the sound of a buzzer. The child engages in hypothesis testing and uses the chime-buzzer for feedback regarding the soundness of a particular problem-solving strategy.

The *Tactual Performance Test* (TPT) measures sensorimotor ability and manual dexterity in the context of tactile form discrimination. Materials consist of a board with six indented geometric shapes and corresponding blocks. The child is blindfolded and attempts to place the blocks in the correct holes, first with the dominant hand, then with the nondominant hand, and finally with both hands. With the blindfold removed, the child is asked to draw a picture of the board. Scores relate to the time needed to complete these trials.

The *Seashore Rhythm Test* measures auditory alertness, sustained attention, and rhythmic sequence discrimination. The child is presented with 30 pairs of rhythm sequences and has to indicate whether the pairs are the same or different.

The *Speech-Sounds Perception Test* assesses auditory perception and auditory-visual integration. The child is presented with a number of tape-recorded nonsense words. He or she must indicate which one of four choices of spellings most resembles the spoken word.

The *Finger Tapping Test* measures fine motor speed. Using the index finger, the child is asked to tap as quickly as possible the lever of a specially adapted counter. The dominant hand is used for five 10-second trials and the nondominant hand is used for five more 10-second trials.

The *Strength of Grip Test* measures strength of upper extremities. The child is asked to squeeze the Smedley Hand Dynamometer as hard as possible with alternating trials for each hand.

The *Trail Making Test* requires visual scanning, sequential processing, and an appreciation of the symbolic significance of letters and numbers. It is composed of two parts. Part A consists of 15 numbered circles scattered on a plain sheet of paper. The child connects the dots with a pencil in sequence as quickly as possible. Part B consists of eight circles numbered one to eight and seven circles lettered A to G. For this part, the child connects the circles alternating in proper sequence between numbers and letters.

The *Aphasia Screening Test* screens for receptive and expressive language and spatial processing problems. The child is asked to perform a number of spelling, reading, naming, copying, and computational tasks. Failures are interpreted as representing specific processing deficits.

The *Lateral Dominance Examination* assesses right–left preference through a number of measured activities including name writing.

The complete Halstead Neuropsychological Test Battery for children also includes a number of sensory-perceptual tasks. One task, the *Sensory Imperception Test*, assesses sensory-perceptual abilities. Tactile, auditory, and visual sensory modalities are tested separately. For each, bilateral stimulation is alternated with unilateral stimulation. For all of these tests the score is the number of errors for each side of the body (i.e., sensory suppressions).

The *Tactile Finger Recognition Test* measures sensory skills. The blindfolded child is asked to tell the examiner by name or prearranged system which finger was touched. During the course of this test each finger on both hands is touched four times.

The *Fingertip Number Writing Perception Test* measures sensory-perceptual ability. The blindfolded child is asked to identify a number (3,4,5, or 6) "written" on his or her fingertip. The numbers are presented in a set sequence with four trials for each finger on each hand.

The *Tactile Form Recognition Test* also measures sensory-perceptual ability. The child is asked to identify flat plastic shapes (circle, square, triangle, and cross) using only tactual cues. The answer is indicated nonverbally by the child's pointing to the correct stimulus figure.

The younger children's battery, the Reitan-Indiana Neuropsychological Test Battery for Children, makes use of several of the tests from the older children's battery and adds several unique tests.

The *Category Test* makes use of colored answer buttons instead of numbered ones and uses five sets of slides. In addition, problem-solving strategies are simplified. The *Tactual Performance Test* changes the orientation of the formboard from vertical to horizontal. The *Finger Tapping Test* uses an electric counter rather than a manual one. The *Strength of Grip Test* remains the same as does the *Lateral Dominance Examination*. Several of the *Sensory-Perceptual Measures* reduce verbal response demands. Also, *Fingertip Number Writing* is replaced by *Fingertip Symbol Writing*, using X's and O's instead of numbers.

Five tests are unique to this younger children's battery:

The *Color Form Test* is analogous to the Trail Making Test, Part B, from the older children's battery. It measures thinking flexibility, abstraction, and sequencing. The child is shown a test form with different geometric shapes in different colors and is asked to connect the figures alternating between shape and color.

The *Progressive Figures Test* also measures thinking flexibility and abstraction. The child is asked to connect a series of geometric shapes on the basis of what smaller geometric shape appears within a larger geometric shape. For example, a large triangle with a small circle inside would be connected to a large circle.

The *Matching Pictures Test* measures visual discrimination and conceptual thinking. The child is asked to match pictures at the top of the page with pictures at the bottom. Initial trials make use of exact matching and later trials make use of conceptual matching.

The *Target Test* measures short-term visual recall and visual-spatial organization. Using a 3 × 3 array of dots, the child is asked to duplicate a series of increasingly complicated designs demonstrated first by the examiner.

The *Individual Performance Test* comprises four parts, two requiring visual-motor integration ("Star" and "Concentric Squares") and two requiring visual discrimination ("Matching V's" and "Matching Figures"). For the Star, the child is shown and asked to copy a star made of two overlapping triangles; for the Concentric Squares, the procedure is the same but the stimulus consists of three boxes arranged inside one another. For Matching V's and Matching Figures the child matches blocks to stimuli presented on a cardboard strip.

The *Marching Test*, has two parts and assesses visual-motor coordination and motor planning. For part one, the child "marches" up a sheet of paper with crayon, marking a series of connected circles. This part consists of five sheets, each with an increasingly complex pattern of circles and each with two columns of circles, one for the left hand and one for the right. Part two involves the child's "marching" his or her fingers in a pattern led by the examiner. The child places his or her index fingers in the circles just vacated by the examiner.

The Halstead Neuropsychological Test Battery for Children and the Reitan-Indiana Neuropsychological Test Battery for Children are individually administered and require testing time of 4 to 6 hours each. Frequently, more than one testing session is necessary. Because of the complexities involved in these batteries as well as in the field of clinical neuropsychology itself, some authorities assert that one year or more of intense training in clinical neuropsychology is necessary for minimal competence.[7] Necessary equipment is expensive and bulky, which along with training requisites, makes the availability of these batteries typically limited to hospitals, graduate-level training programs, and individual psychologists specializing in clinical neuropsychology.

The actual administration of the battery can be done by a well-trained technician familiar with the test equipment and the standardized administration procedures described in the manual. Interpretation of obtained data is performed by the psychologist.

Reitan advocates an interpretive strategy that makes use of four methods of neuropsychological inference.[6] The first method, level of performance, compares a child's scores on the various measures to normative standards. Selz and Reitan[4] have developed a system of rules for converting raw scores into scaled scores for this purpose. This process is similar to the sort of interpretive process used for most psychological tests. However, problems such as socioeconomic deprivation, emotional interference, and likely lack of information about a child's previous level of functioning limits the usefulness of this method. Consequently, other interpretive methods less influenced by these potentially confounding variables are used. For example, the pattern of scores (i.e., relative strengths and weaknesses) may be of more significance than the total score. Thus, examining the pattern of performance may lead to diagnostic hypotheses.

Another interpretive strategy relies on the fact that several of the Halstead tests can be used to compare performance on the left side of the body with performance on the right side. Knowledge of the contralateral organization of motor and sensory functions, and the performance advantage typically seen on the dominant side, allows for an understanding of the lateralization of neurological dysfunction.

Finally, failure on some of the Halstead-Reitan tests is seen as providing evidence of brain damage since these tests are designed so that a neurologically intact child should make no errors. These presumably pathognomonic signs are seen on the sensory-perceptual tasks and on the Aphasia Screening Test. It should be noted, however, that a child's failure on the Aphasia Screening Test is less clearly an unequivocal sign of brain damage than an adult's failure since educational experiences, motivation, or socioeconomic factors can affect performance. Therefore, a child's failure on the Aphasia Screening Test should be interpreted with caution.

The Halstead-Reitan batteries have several practical limitations.[1] The materials are expensive and not portable and administration time is rather lengthy. Patients with overt, preexisting sensory and/or motor handicaps cannot be thoroughly examined. Further, there is no clear agreement on standard age norms. Interpretation, then, can sometimes be more subjective than objective.

The actual utility of the Halstead-Reitan batteries remains difficult to assess. Some, including Rutter,[8] claim limited usefulness, especially for diagnosing neurological damage in children with learning disabilities. Sattler[2] notes poorly developed and limited age norms. Others[1,3] however, see the Halstead-Reitan batteries as quite effective in differentiating patients with brain damage. The validity studies have shown consistently that groups of children with known brain damage score lower on the neuropsychological measures than groups of age-matched controls. Studies looking at the Halstead-Reitan batteries for localizing damage have had equivocal results,[1] and one reviewer considers information about the reliability and validity of these batteries scarce.[3]

Considering the limitations of the Halstead-Reitan batteries, the greatest usefulness may not be in diagnosis and localization of brain damage but in remediational applications. Objective baseline data serve to clarify a child's neuropsychological assets and liabilities. This information can be extremely valuable to a child and his or her family in understanding the implications of the brain damage and can guide educators in designing educational programs specific to a child's pattern of strengths and weaknesses.

CASE ILLUSTRATION

Michael H., 9 years, 5 months old, was referred for psychological evaluation because of academic underachievement. The results of the evaluation revealed average intellectual functioning on the Wechsler Intelligence Scale for Children (Full Scale IQ = 92) but with a statistically significant difference between his Verbal IQ score (102), and his Performance IQ score (84). Of further concern was the variability among Performance subtest scores which ranged from average to more than 2 standard deviations below average. Neuropsychological testing was recommended by the examining psychologist to elaborate these findings and aid in intervention planning.

Tests administered were the Halstead-Reitan Neuropsychological Test Battery for Children and the Bender Visual Motor Gestalt Test (Chapters 9 and 8, respectively). Michael cooperated fully but appeared somewhat sad and frightened.

Analysis of the Bender and the previously administered WISC–R indicated serious processing problems in visual-spatial reasoning as well as visual-motor integration and coordination. Neuropsychological test battery results indicated other problems in the motor and tactual areas, as well as difficulties in auditory discrimination. Most of Michael's difficulties were evident in functions mediated by the right cerebral hemisphere. His strength of grip and tapping speed were less than expected with his left hand (based on his right-hand scores), and there were left-hand tactual imperceptions and discrimination errors as well. Additional problems were evident in Michael's decoding of verbal information and in his making accurate auditory discriminations (as reflected by poor showings on the Aphasia Screening Test and Seashore Rhythm Test). On the positive side, Michael's good scores on Categories, Trails, and the WISC–R Coding subtests contraindicated the presence of an ongoing degenerative cerebral process and indicated that he does have well-developed skills in complex problem solving and sequencing.

Recommendations from the neuropsychological testing focused on Michael's need for an educational program that addresses his processing deficits and at the same time provides him with a challenge for his above-average skills. It was felt that a specialized classroom for children with learning disabilities would be appropriate for these purposes. Specific recommendations addressed Michael's need for practice in handwriting as well as provision for other channels of responding in subjects such as spelling, where answers could be given orally. Additionally, it was suggested that Michael be encouraged to use a typewriter and/or tape recorder for lengthy homework assignments.

Finally, it was stressed that Michael had been expending considerable amounts of energy on his academic work and that any frustrations or irritability could be reduced by providing an understanding and encouraging atmosphere at school and at home. That is, it was hoped that Michael's academic underachievement would be viewed as a result of neurological dysfunctions and not laziness or stubbornness.

Luria-Nebraska Children's Battery

The Luria-Nebraska Children's Neuropsychological Test Battery assesses brain–behavior relationships in children 8 to 12 years of age.[9] It is based on the neuropsychological and neurodevelopmental theories of A. R. Luria, a Russian physician and psychologist.[10,11,12] Whereas the Halstead-Reitan Batteries focus on specific localization of brain lesions, the Luria-Nebraska Batteries focus on functional systems of neural zones that are involved in brain–behavior relationships. The adult version, the Luria-Nebraska Neuropsychological Battery, has been in use since 1979 and continues to gain considerable attention and acceptance.[13] Unlike some children's versions of adult tests which simply provide downward extensions of the same basic tasks, the Luria-Nebraska Children's Battery takes into account the neurological development of children so that many of the tasks are qualitatively different from those on the adult battery.

The standardization of this battery began by eliminating items from the adult battery that were neurodevelopmentally inappropriate for children (viz., those tapping certain frontal lobe functions). Remaining items were modified to make the materials and instructions appropriate for the intended 8- to 12-year-old age group. Ongoing research has prompted several revisions with the latest (1980) normed on 120 intact children, 24 at each of the five age levels.[9]

The current version of this battery assesses functioning in 11 areas.[9] *Motor Skills* includes speed, coordination, imitation, and construction. Examples include (a) having the child touch his or her fingers in turn with his or her thumb as quickly as possible and (b) drawing a square without lifting the pencil from the paper.

Rhythm Skills assesses auditory discrimination and recall using tones, tunes, and rhythmic patterns. As an example, the child is asked to repeat a series of alternating strong and weak taps demonstrated by the examiner.

Tactile Skills includes two-point discrimination, finger and arm localization, movement detection, shape discrimination, and strength discrimination. In one item, the blindfolded child is asked whether he or she is being touched with the head or point of a pin. A series of touches (heads and points alternating) are presented for each hand.

Visual Skills is concerned with basic visual recognition of real objects and pictures. *Receptive Speech Skills* assesses the child's understanding of words and simple commands. *Expressive Language Skills* looks at the child's ability to read and repeat sounds and words and to name objects from visual and oral descriptions.

Writing Skills involves the child's writing letters and letter sequences from visual and vocal sources. *Reading Skills* involves the child's reading letters, nonsense syllables, words, sentences, and paragraphs. *Arithmetic Skills* involves number recognition, writing, and comparisons as well as basic numerical reasoning and computation.

The *Memory Skills* items assess verbal and nonverbal short-term recall. Some of the tasks employ interference strategies. *Intelligence* items are similar to items contained in the Similarities, Arithmetic, Vocabulary, Comprehension, Picture Completion, and Picture Arrangement subtests of the Wechsler Intelligence Scale for Children—Revised.

The Luria-Nebraska Children's Battery is individually administered by an examiner familiar with Luria's neuropsychological theory and well acquainted with the battery's materials, intricate administration procedures, and scoring rules. It is best used for evaluating children with known or suspected brain damage in order to support or clarify other neurological findings and to provide baseline data against which future evaluations can be made. This battery is used typically in hospital and clinic settings.

Scoring of test items is based on normative data for the 8- to 12-year-old age group. A three-point system has been established whereby a score of 0 is given for performance equal to or less than 1 standard deviation below the mean, a score of 1 for performance between 1 and 2 standard deviations below the mean, and a score of 2 for performance more than 2 standard deviations below the mean. A score for each of the 11 scales is determined by adding the item scores comprising the scale. With tables provided in the test booklet, these scores are transformed into standard *t* scores with a mean of 50 and a standard deviation of 10.

Compared to the Halstead-Reitan batteries, the Luria battery takes less time (two hours), has simpler procedures for the patient, and requires less cumbersome materials. However, proper administration is quite intricate and requires much training. Some portions of the battery require subjective judgments regarding certain procedures. Scoring, however, is straightforward and objective. The battery cannot be used with children who have sensory or motor handicaps.

Because research on the Luria Children's Battery began only in 1980,[13] a large body of validative research has not yet accumulated. However, initial studies suggest that the battery effectively predicts IQ and reading levels.[9] Additionally, children with documented brain damage have been shown to perform significantly poorer than matched intact controls.[9] It should be noted that the neurodevelopmental basis of the battery does not allow for the identification of children with damage to the tertiary frontal areas of the brain.

Proponents of this battery are optimistic that its reliance on Luria's neuropsychological theories will become a significant addition to child assessment procedures.[13] Preliminary research is promising, but more extensive research is needed to verify the battery's clinical utility.

ACKNOWLEDGMENTS

Special thanks to Anne M. Sitarz, PhD, for her contributions to this chapter.

References

1. Lezak MD: *Neuropsychological Assessment.* New York, Oxford University Press, 1976.
2. Sattler JM: *Assessment of Children's Intelligence and Special Abilities,* ed 2. Boston, Allyn & Bacon Inc, 1982.
3. Selz M: Halstead-Reitan Neuropsychological Test Batteries for Children, in Hynd GW, Obrzut JE (eds): *Neuropsychological Assessment and the School Aged Child.* New York, Grune & Stratton, 1982.
4. Selz M, Reitan RM: Rules for neuropsychological diagnosis: Classification of brain function in older children. *Consulting and Clinical Psychology* 47:258–264, 1979.
5. Halstead WC: *Brain and Intelligence.* Chicago, University of Chicago Press, 1947.
6. Reitan RM, Davisson LA (eds): *Clinical Neuropsychology: Current Status and Implications.* Washington, DC, VH Winston and Sons, 1974.
7. Rourke BP: Issues in the neuropsychological assessment of children with learning disabilities. *Canadian Psychological Review* 17:89–102, 1976.
8. Rutter M: Psychological sequelae of brain damage in children. *Am J Psychiatry* 138:1533–1544, 1981.
9. Golden CJ: *Luria-Nebraska Neuropsychological Battery for Children.* Unpublished experimental test form, University of Nebraska, 1980.
10. Luria AR: *Higher Cortical Functions in Man.* New York, Basic Books, 1966.
11. Luria AR: *The Working Brain.* New York, Basic Books, 1973.
12. Christensen AL: *Luria's Neuropsychological Investigation.* New York, Spectrum, 1975.
13. Golden CJ: The Luria-Nebraska Children's Battery: Theory and formulation, in Hynd GW & Obrzut JE (eds): *Neuropsychological Assessment and the School-Age Child.* New York, Grune & Stratton, 1982.

Chapter 10

Tests of Social/Adaptive Skills

Tests of Social and Adaptive Skills

Definitions of adaptive behavior include behavior that is instrumental in meeting the demands of one's natural and social environments.[1] Definitions and assessment strategies must take into account developmental and cultural perspectives. The developmental perspective is essential since there are different expectations regarding what individuals should be able to do independently as they develop. Adaptive behavior definitions also must take into account cultural variables since cultures differ regarding what they expect from individuals in terms of personal and social responsibility.

Although intelligence and adaptation are related, correlations are not strong enough to allow one to be predicted from the other. Frequently, inner-city or rural children in poverty conditions who are referred for assessment because of school failure evidence subaverage intelligence but quite adequate adjustment to the demands of their environments.

The American Association on Mental Deficiency has presented guidelines for the use of measures of adaptive behavior when mental retardation is suspected.[1] These guidelines have influenced the diagnostic criteria for mental retardation that appear in the American Psychiatric Association's *Diagnostic and Statistical Manual of Mental*

Disorders (3rd ed).[2] According to the DSM-III, for an individual to be diagnosed as mentally retarded he or she must show significantly subaverage intellectual functioning, onset before the age of 18 years, and "concurrent deficits or impairments in [age-appropriate] adaptive behavior."[2] Also influencing contemporary notions of the importance of assessing adaptive behavior are the guidelines for the assessment of mentally retarded individuals that appear in the Education for All Handicapped Children Act (Public Act 94-142, Federal Register, 1977). The passage of this law has led to most states' developing guidelines stressing the assessment of adaptive behavior.[3 (p 311)]

There are a number of instruments useful for assessing adaptive behavior. The following two sections present the most widely used instruments, the Vineland Social Maturity Scale[4] and the American Association on Mental Deficiency Adaptive Behavior Scale.[5] A case illustration accompanies the section on the Vineland.

The American Association on Mental Deficiency Adaptive Behavior Scale

The American Association on Mental Deficiency Adaptive Behavior Scale (ABS) is a behavior rating scale that assesses behavioral and adaptive competencies in developmentally disabled, mentally retarded, and emotionally disturbed individuals.[5] The ABS was originally published in 1969 and revised in 1974. The American Association on Mental Deficiency (AAMD), through which the ABS was developed, has been instrumental in refining definitions of adaptive behavior, in developing methods of assessing adaptive behavior, and in clarifying the implications of such assessment.

The ABS contains two parts. The first portion comprises the behavior domains and assesses ten survival skills and habits seen as important in independent daily living. These ten behavioral domains include independent functioning (e.g., eating, toileting, appearance), physical development, economic activity, language development, numbers and time, domestic activity, vocational activity, self-direction, responsibility, and socialization.

The second portion of the ABS focuses on maladaptive behaviors. It includes 14 behaviors related to personality and behavior disorders: violent/destructive behaviors, antisocial behavior, rebellious behavior, untrustworthy behavior, withdrawal, stereotyped behavior/odd mannerisms, inappropriate interpersonal manners, unacceptable vocal habits, unacceptable or eccentric habits, self-abusive behavior, hyperactive tendencies, sexually aberrant behavior, psychological disturbances, and use of medications.

The ABS is used most commonly with institutionalized individuals. In such settings the ABS is useful in helping determine placement within the institution, planning habilitation programs, and assessing changes occurring in treatment. As a criterion-referenced procedure, the ABS is useful in understanding variability and changes in an individual's functioning. Unlike a normative-referenced procedure, the ABS gives minimal importance to comparisons with other individuals.

This scale can be administered by individuals with little formal training. The construction of test questions makes scoring simple and objective. Administration time is 15 to 30 minutes. The interviewer goes through the various items with a person familiar with the patient in order to make the necessary ratings. The informants can be the patient's parents, ward attendants, nurses, or other involved health professionals. For both parts of the scale raw scores for the various items comprising the domains are translated into percentile-based standard scores. The manual provides these scores for 11 age groups ranging from 3 years to 69 years of age. Habilitation planning proceeds by analyzing the individual's strengths and weaknesses. Even in highly impaired individuals relative strengths can be used strategically to compensate or bolster weaknesses or to help modify unacceptable behaviors (those evidenced in Part II of the scale).

A version of the ABS was restandardized for use in public schools in 1975.[6] The resulting AAMD–ABS Public School Version (ABS–PSV) is used with children 7 years, 3 months to 13 years, 2 months. It is identical to the original ABS except for the elimination of some of the domains not applicable to school settings (Part I eliminated domestic activity; Part II eliminated self-abusive and sexually aberrant behavior). Administration is similar to the ABS; parents and teachers are encouraged to fill out the record forms. Reviews of the ABS–PSV point out adequate reliability but questionable validity for the school-age groups it serves.[3] The ABS–PSV has been seen as useful for the purposes of profiling adaptive behavior strengths and weaknesses and developing intervention plans. However, it has been criticized as being inappropriate for physically handicapped, emotionally disturbed, or underprivileged children.[3]

The original ABS was standardized on mentally retarded individuals. Interrater reliability is acceptable. Although validity has been established within the scale, discrepancies have occurred when ABS ratings were compared with those obtained on other behavior rating scales.[7]

The usefulness of the ABS is clear among institutionalized mentally retarded individuals. Clear descriptions of daily living skills and social behavior are obtained. It can also be used to develop training strategies and trace progress in treatment. The limited standardization group and not fully established validity data have led some researchers to conclude that placement decisions and behavioral statements should be made in conjunction with scores obtained on additional instruments.[7]

Vineland Social Maturity Scale and Vineland Adaptive Behavior Scales

The Vineland Social Maturity Scale[4] is the best known and most widely used measure of social competence. It assesses self-help skills, self-direction, and responsibility in individuals from birth to maturity. The scale was first published in 1935 with revisions appearing in 1947, 1953, and 1965. A technical manual, *The Measurement of Social Competence: A Manual for the Vineland Social Maturity Scale*[8] was initially published in 1953. A completely reconceptualized and restandardized version of the Vineland was published in 1984 as the Vineland Adaptive Behavior Scales.[9]

The original Vineland was standardized on 620 white male and female residents of New Jersey, including 10 males and 10 females at each year of age from birth to 30 years. The scale consists of 117 items arranged serially in increasingly difficult order. Placement of items is based on the results of original normative studies with each item assigned a Life Age (LA) score representing the average age when the item was achieved by the standardization sample.

The Vineland's items cluster into eight categories:

1. *Self-help, General:* Fourteen items that assess early physical maturation, mobility, toileting, and telling time from .25 years to 7.28 years (e.g., balances head, tells time to the quarter hour).
2. *Self-help, Eating:* Twelve items assessing the mechanics of eating from .55 years to 9.03 years (e.g., drinks from cup unassisted, cares for self at table).
3. *Self-help, Dressing:* Thirteen items focusing on dressing and bathing skills from 1.13 years to 12.38 years (e.g., pulls off socks, takes complete care of dress).
4. *Locomotion:* Ten items that assess directed movement from .63 years to 18.5 years (e.g., crawls, travels to distant towns).

5. *Occupation*: Twenty-two items assessing productive use of time from .43 to 25+ years (e.g., occupies self unattended, creates own opportunities.)
6. *Communication*: Fifteen items focusing on conveying and receiving information from .25 years to 15.35 years (e.g., crows and laughs, follows current events).
7. *Self-direction*: Fourteen items that assess taking financial and personal responsibility from 5.83 years to 25+ years (e.g., is trusted with money, makes purchases for others).
8. *Socialization*: Seventeen items assessing relationships with others from .30 years to 25+ years (e.g., reaches for familiar persons, advances general welfare).

Although the Vineland is not an intelligence test, it can be used to obtain developmental data when a child is unresponsive, uncooperative, or unavailable for direct assessment. More commonly the Vineland provides data about a child's adaptive behavior for purposes of diagnosing mental retardation when the IQ test score falls in the mentally deficient range. The Vineland is used in a broad variety of medical, mental health, and educational settings.

The administration of the Vineland requires a qualified examiner familiar with the scale items and interview procedures. Administration time is 20 to 30 minutes and typically uses the child's parent or major caretaker as informant. In a structured interview format, the examiner determines how the child usually performs the particular behavior. A "pass" is given only when it is judged that the child *usually performs* the particular activity, not for those activities that the child is capable of performing. The interview proceeds from one category of behavior to another. A basal score and a ceiling score are obtained in each category with the basal determined as two consecutive passes and the ceiling defined as two consecutive failures. Scoring rules allow the child not to be penalized for temporary or circumstantial failures and limited opportunities to perform the activity. The total number of passed items is converted into a standard score or social age (SA) using a table in the manual. A ratio social quotient (SQ) can be calculated by dividing the child's SA by his or her chronological age and then multiplying by 100. For more statistically accurate scores, a deviation SQ can be determined with a table developed by Silverstein.[10]

Although the actual items on the Vineland seem clear and unambiguous, some are misleading and must be fully understood by the examiner so that accurate determinations can be made. Otherwise, inexperienced examiners may obtain inflated scores. The scale can be used with physically handicapped children although care should be taken that the child is not penalized for not being able to perform certain activities because of the handicapping condition. Resultant scores must be interpreted with caution.

The test–retest reliability of the Vineland has been shown to be satisfactory.[8] However, teachers and mothers have been shown to differ in their ratings of the same children with mothers typically reporting higher SQs.[11] The Vineland correlates moderately with measures of development and intelligence.[12]

Although the Vineland has been viewed as a valuable clinical tool[13,14] critics have focused on its limited psychometric properties, out-of-date standardization data,[3] [(p 316)] and limited use with handicapped children.

The major revision of the Vineland[9] addresses some of these criticisms and may become even more useful than the original. The new Vineland Adaptive Behavior Scales[9] comprise three distinct scales: two interview scales (one brief scale and a longer one suited to institutional programming purposes) and one checklist for use by teachers. These scales assess adaptive functioning in individuals from birth to 19 years (and low functioning adults). The teacher scale is used for children 3 to 13 years. Adaptive functioning is assessed in five domains: communication, daily living skills, socialization, motor skills, and maladaptive behavior. The classroom scale assesses the first four of these domains.

A stratified national sample was used for standardization data.[9] This normative research was conducted in conjunction with the standardization work done for the Kaufman Assessment Battery for Children (see Chapter 7). The Vineland Adaptive Behavior Scales make provisions for specialized interpretation of handicapped children. Separate scales were developed for hearing-impaired, visually impaired, and emotionally disturbed children in residential settings.

Although clinical and research experiences will have to accumulate before firm conclusions can be drawn regarding the usefulness of these new scales, preliminary impressions are quite promising in terms of answering the major criticisms directed toward the original Vineland.

CASE ILLUSTRATION

Paul A. is a 4½-year-old boy referred for a psychological evaluation by his nursery school teacher and pediatrician. Paul was described as not acquiring preschool academic readiness skills as quickly as his schoolmates. Behaviorally he was seen as shy, clinging to adults, and shunning peers.

During psychological testing Paul was a friendly and engaging youngster. His tolerance for frustration was quite low, frequently giving up when meeting difficulty. The results of testing included intellectual functioning in the average range, with a Stanford-Binet Mental Age of 4 years, 9 months, and IQ of 95. Further, there was no indication of particular intellectual weaknesses.

As part of the evaluation, the Vineland Social Maturity Scale was administered, with Paul's mother serving as informant. The resulting score produced a social age of 3 years, 7 months and a social quotient of 80. Specific areas in which Paul's mother reported less than age-appropriate functioning included Self-help, General; Self-help, Eating; and, Self-help, Dressing.

The discrepancy between Paul's intellectual capabilities and social competence suggested that he could have been functioning at a higher level of independence given proper opportunities. Further discussion with Mrs. A. revealed her to possess an overprotective and infantilizing attitude toward Paul. It was concluded that Paul's behavior and achievement in school were influenced by his mother's attitudes and behavior. The psychologist recommended child-oriented parent guidance for Mrs. A. along with consultation with Paul's nursery school teacher.

References

1. Grossman HJ: *Manual on Terminology and Classification in Mental Retardation (1973 revision)*. American Association on Mental Deficiency. Baltimore, Garamond/Pridemark Press, 1973.
2. American Psychiatric Association: *Diagnostic and Statistical Manual of Mental Disorders*, (ed 3). Washington, DC, APA, 1980, p 40.
3. Sattler JM: *Assessment of Children's Intelligence and Special Abilities* (ed 2). Boston, Allyn and Bacon, Inc, 1982.
4. Doll EA: *Vineland Social Maturity Scale. Birth to Maturity*. Minneapolis, Educational Test Bureau, 1935–1953.
5. Nihira K, Foster R, Shellhaas M, Leland H: *AAMD Adaptive Behavior Scale (rev ed)*. Washington, DC, American Association on Mental Deficiency, 1974.
6. Lambert NM, Windmiller M, Cole L, Figueroa RA: Standardization of a public school version of the AAMD Adaptive Behavior Scale. *Mental Retardation* 13, 1975, 3–7.
7. Millham J, Chilcutt J, Atkinson B: Criterion validity of the AAMD Adaptive Behavior Scale. In Millham J (chair) *Reliability and Validity of the Adaptive Behavior Scales*, Symposium presented at the meeting of the American Psychological Association, Washington, DC, Sept 1978.
8. Doll EA: *The Measurement of Social Competence. A Manual for the Vineland Social Maturity Scale*. Philadelphia, Educational Test Bureau, Educational Publishers, 1953.

9. Sparrow S, Balla D, Cicchetti DV: *Vineland Adaptive Behavior Scales.* Circle Pines, MN, American Guidance Service, 1984.
10. Silverstein AB: Deviation social quotients for the Vineland Social Maturity Scale. *Am J Mental Deficiency* 76:348–351, 1971.
11. Kaplan HE, Alatishe M: Comparison of ratings by mothers and teachers on preschool children using the Vineland Social Maturity Scale. *Psychology in the Schools* 13:27–28, 1976.
12. Krasner BR, Silverstein L: The Preschool Attainment Record: A concurrent validity study with cerebral palsied children. *Educational and Psychological Measurement* 36:1049–1054, 1976.
13. Teagarden FM: Review of the Vineland Social Maturity Scale. In Buros OK (ed) *Fourth Mental Measurements Yearbook.* Highland Park, NJ, Gryphon Press, 1953, pp 162–163.
14. Watson RI: *The Clinical Method in Psychology.* New York, Harper, 1951.

Chapter 11

Personality Inventories and Projective Measures

In order to study and measure personality, regardless of theoretical orientation, methods of assessing personality variables are necessary. There are today literally hundreds of different tests available for psychologists to use in assessing personality differences. The tests vary from objective self-report questionnaires to tests which emphasize personal style and expression. Techniques such as inkblots, story telling, figure drawings, play construction, reactions to humor, adjective descriptions, and role playing have all been used as means by which to gather information about an individual's personality makeup.

This section discusses five types of tests which have been most familiar to the clinician and are perhaps the most popular ways of detecting personality styles and psychopathology. Methods such as figure drawings and sentence completions represent, among other attributes, an effective means for "breaking the ice" during the initial moments between the examiner and child. These tasks are generally intrinsically interesting, often entertaining, and provide minimal threat to the child since there are no wrong or right answers. Projective techniques such as the Thematic Apperception Test, the Children's Apperception Test, and the Rorschach are less structured, more ambiguous approaches which assume that the child "projects" his or her own personality onto the stimulus. Projectives tap the child's imagination and the way in which he or she perceives and interprets the test materials or structures the situation. They are thought to reflect basic aspects of psychological functioning. Personality inventories (e.g., the MMPI) strive for objectivity in that they are easily scored and can be evaluated for reliability and validity. Because of their rigid structure whereby responses are limited to one of several presented answers, however, these methods severely restrict flexible and spontaneous expression.

House–Tree–Person and Family Drawings

The use of projective drawings has evolved rapidly as an important element in the psychological test battery. Because of their brevity, non-threatening nature, ease of administration, and vast interpretive product, projective drawings appear to be the most frequent adjunct to the Rorschach and TAT in the everyday tools of the clinician whose concern is personality assessment.[1,2] Besides their use in assisting in the diagnostic process, they have also been incorporated as vital aids in psychotherapy, especially with children and withdrawn individuals. Drawings have also been used advantageously as a screening device in evaluating a child's adjustment before entering school or special training programs.

Unlike the adult who may become defensive when asked to draw objects, a child's response is usually quite positive, with little noticeable tension. For the child, drawings become vehicles for expression of fears, wish fulfilments, and fantasies. It is also likely that the drawings become means by which the child can deal with frustrations and impulses. Viewed in this manner, the drawings become highly meaningful and communicative for the child.

The typical request from the clinician is to draw a house, a tree, and a person. These three entities are chosen because of their familiarity to children of all ages, their acceptance in comparison with other possible objects, and their ability to stimulate freer expressions than other items. Each of the drawings is analyzed for certain characteristics. For example, an analysis focuses on both the structural features of the drawing (size, background, placement on page, etc.) and the content (e.g., individual body parts and posture for the person.)

Both the House–Tree–Person and Draw-A-Person procedures, as personality instruments, were initially developed from intellectual tests. Florence Goodenough[3] constructed a measure of children's intelligence based primarily on the quantity of details placed into the drawing of a man (see section on Draw-A-Person). Later she and other clinicians became aware of the possibilities that these drawings were tapping features of the child's personality along with mental endowment. The

Figure Drawing device,[4] in fact, was developed out of the exposure with the Goodenough instrument. In a similiar manner, the House–Tree–Person[5] developed as an ancillary of an intellectual test which was being constructed during the time Wechsler produced his original intellectual scale. The Family Drawing procedure, by contrast, is a more recent phenomenon which seems to have become popular with the advent of family treatment. This informative device came into being so quickly that its authorship remains unknown.[1]

Drawings for clinical use serve as projective techniques because they confront the child with situations which are unstructured. This requires that the child derive meaning for the task from his or her own experience. The ambiguity in the task lies in the minimal direction provided by the examiner. The child is not told what to draw and can respond in an infinite arrangement as to the size, placement, age, and so on of each drawing. Much like story-telling tests in which themes are derived, the child primarily selects traits or situations from previous experiences which reflect personal needs.

It is assumed that each of the drawings taps different areas of personality. The House, for example, is usually viewed as stimulating associations regarding family ties, and conflicts surrounding the home life. For children, much of the focus in this kind of drawing is based on perceptions of parents and siblings. This is also true of the Family Drawing where the main principle in its use is to ascertain the salience of the child's perceived relationship within the family structure. Of particular importance is how the child views himself or herself in relation to the parents and siblings. For instance, a child who has greater status within the family will likely place himself or herself much closer to or on the same level with the parents. In contrast, a child who feels isolated or different in some manner might draw himself or herself at a distance or as not participating in a family activity.

Concerning the Tree and Person, many theorists have suggested that these concepts are directly or indirectly connected with the child's body image and self-concept. Of the two, the Tree is regarded as reflecting deeper and more unaware personal feelings. For the child, it is easier to ascribe a greater amount of less desirable traits to a tree, since it appears more removed from a description of self. By contrast, the drawing of a person becomes a more direct expression of real-life feelings concerning self and interpersonal comparisons.

Each of the drawings may be considered within the context of a self-portrait reflecting a variety of characteristics, such as the child's feelings of adequacy and contentment, accessibility, degree of reality testing, and sexual role. For instance, the correspondence between the size of the drawings and the available space appears to indicate a perception of self-worth (i.e., smallness related to inadequacy, large drawing corresponding to expansiveness and aggression).

The behavior of the child during the drawings yields as much information as the actual production. The careful examiner can observe the child's handedness, motor dexterity, orientation when confronted with an unstructured test, reluctance or eagerness in pursuing the task, dependency needs, impulsivity, tenseness, and insecurities. It is at this stage that initial impressions are formed and hypotheses generated which further testing and analysis will confirm or reject. Although interpretation varies based on knowledge of previous research and personal experiences, deductions must be made cautiously and viewed within the larger scope of the existing information.

CASE ILLUSTRATIONS

The following remarks about a series of figures show possible interpretive avenues open to the clinician for hypotheses and exploration. They could not be considered at all definitive until supported by additional clinical data such as more rigorous projective techniques, parent and child interviews, and observation sessions. Each figure drawn by a child (or adult) has an array of possible meanings and interpretations. Only a few comments concerning each of the figures can be offered in the space available.

The house in Figure 13, drawn by a 12-year-old boy who had recently been sexually molested, suggested the guarded and suspicious manner in which he approached the psychological testing. The shades on each of the windows probably exemplified his nervousness at being in a room alone with the male examiner and uncertainty about how much to reveal. The path leading to the bottom of the paper seemed to be an anchor for him, again reflecting his insecurities and perceived need to maintain psychological distance.

The house in Figure 14, drawn by an 8-year-old girl whose father had been murdered in the house, has several salient features. The intensity of her anxiety and inability to understand the event are represented by the shading of the roof. The three windows of decreasing size probably symbolize the remaining members of the household (mother, patient, brother).

The tree in Figure 15, remarkable for its sketchiness, absence of roots and ground line, and the knothole above the middle of the trunk, was drawn by a 14-year-old boy who was a product of multiple placements after age 8 and whose behavior was characterized by volatile outbursts and impulsivity. The height of the tree is

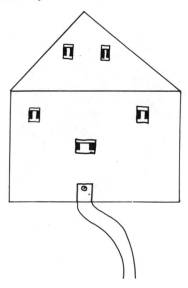

Figure 13. House drawn by a 12-year-old boy.

Figure 14. House drawn by an 8-year-old girl.

sometimes considered to represent age, with the placement of the knothole symbolizing the time of a traumatic event.[5] The sketchy lines are typically viewed as indicating a high degree of anxiety.

The tree in Figure 16, drawn by an overly aggressive 12-year-old boy, attests to his pointed anger and his high degree of activity and expansiveness (the picture covered the entire page). The thorny branches could be a warning to others to keep their distance. The tree is also suggestive of a highly anxious, empty individual who

Figure 15. Tree drawn by a 14-year-old boy.

Figure 16. Tree drawn by a 12-year-old boy.

is experiencing sexual concerns or is yearning for something or someone powerful. The lack of leaves and absence of earth line attest to the child's minimal feelings of warmth and sensitivity.

The most salient aspect of the drawing in Figure 17 is its absence of hands and feet. This is often indicative of feelings of helplessness and dependency which were certainly present in the 14-year-old girl who made this drawing. Some authors[6] have suggested that since these two parts of the body are difficult to draw, persons who are sensitive about their abilities tend to bypass these features because they may not be able to succeed. The picture also shows arms close to the side of the body and a large open mouth, together suggesting dependency, shyness, and possible lack of assertiveness.

The drawing in Figure 18, constructed by an 8-year-old boy who was referred to an outpatient psychiatric center by his school for behavioral and academic problems, reflected an accurate representation of the family structure (which was later confirmed in family therapy sessions). The oldest brother, represented in the top drawing, was certainly the most powerful and stabilizing person in the family. In this drawing, he was portrayed as a boxer (which he was at an amateur level), signifying his potency and superiority.

It was interesting to note the inner triangle between the mother, father, and patient and the proximity of the patient to the mother (perhaps oedipal conflicts). Also, the father was represented in a

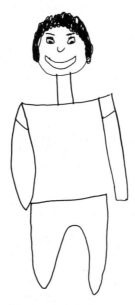

Figure 17. Figure made by a 14-year-old girl.

Figure 18. Family drawing made by an 8-year-old boy.

very passive posture and isolated (the outline of the bed) from the rest of the family (a true description). The mother (the central figure in the family) was placed in the middle of the picture and was the only person drawn with hands (she was the main disciplinarian and was physical in her punishment). The drawing also acknowledged the high activity level of this family.

The developmentally immature nature of the figures and the lack of bodies were noteworthy. Sometimes children draw stick figures when they do not wish to, or cannot, reveal certain aspects of themselves.

The family drawing in Figure 19 was completed by a 6½-year-old boy referred by his pediatrician because of possible learning delays and concomitant emotional problems. This child, the oldest

Figure 19. Family drawing made by a 6½-year-old boy.

of four children, did not include himself (or the youngest sister) in the picture although he placed an odd looking "Humpty Dumpty" character as a central figure in the drawing. It is probable that this character was a reflection of his poor self-image and sensitivity to feeling different from the other family members, as he had been constantly teased by his younger siblings. Recalling the story of Humpty Dumpty might make the clinician wonder if this child, too, feared disaster or personal disintegration. The central placement of the figure could also represent the intensity of these feelings and the attention derived by the family's concern. Possible sibling rivalry was also apparent in the distance between this character and the sister and the status he perceived her to possess in the family structure.

Sentence Completion Tests

In completion tests, the individual is usually asked to finish sentences, stories, arguments, or conversations. They can be administered either in group settings or on an individual basis and are used within the psychological test battery to stimulate associations in specific topic areas and to avoid initial resistance. Although these kinds of projective techniques are infrequently used with preadolescents because of the level of verbal sophistication required, there are several well-standardized forms of sentence completion tests developed for adolescents.[7,8] Often with these tests, the individual is generally requested to write the ending to a sentence which begins with a word or phrase, such as "I" or "The happiest time."

This method of enhancing personal disclosure is usually considered to fall between a subjective report of personal attitudes, experiences, and the like and associative methods like the TAT or Rorschach. The simplicity of the method lends itself to the adolescent's usually realizing that the "stems" are directing him or her to express feelings concerning attitudes and family life, but the form is not so visibly structured as to discourage spontaneous associations.[9 (p 135)]

As a typical example, the Rotter Incomplete Sentences Blank—High School Form (RISB–H) will be considered for discussion in this section. The RISB–H consists of 40 incomplete sentences or sentence "stems."[7] The selection of the 40 stems is based on the various areas of possible conflict that adolescents might be experiencing, for example, important differences with parental or peer figures, salient needs, environmental stressors, and aggressive trends.

The RISB–H can be administered either individually or in groups and takes approximately 15–20 minutes to complete. The 40 items are contained on both sides of the record form, which also includes the instructions and spaces for completion of identifying information. Each completion can be rated on a 7-point scale according to the amount of adjustment or maladjustment indicated. The manual contains numerous examples presented as guides for scoring. With the aid of these examples, fairly objective scoring is possible and adequate scoring reliability has been reported.[10]

The RISB was designed to be used largely as a gross screening instrument for maladjustment among college students. It was also intended to be an aid in research and means of gathering information which would aid in diagnosis and treatment. It appears that its best feature, however, is its value for subjective interpretation.[11] As in all projective instruments, interpretation depends on the examiner's general clinical experience, skill, and awareness of personality dynamics.

Since the RISB is primarily self-administered, an individual can complete the form before entering the examination room and it can then be used to help delineate that person's problem areas. Although the statements provide clues to the present functioning of the youth, often adolescents who are well defended may resist revealing themselves in this fashion and may give popular or ambiguous responses.[8] Of course, this style of resistance provides hypotheses regarding the adolescent's level of discomfort and his or her rebelliousness toward authority figures. Another way of noting resistance is to examine the form for items left blank. These "overlooked" items typically suggest a greater degree of conflict occurring in those areas.

CASE ILLUSTRATION

Wayne P., 16 years old, was being evaluated because of frequent temper outbursts and destructive behavior. The juvenile court had decided to send him to an inpatient psychiatric unit for 30 days and not formally adjudicate his case until after a thorough evaluation. Although intelligent (WISC–R = 120), Wayne initially presented as socially awkward, displaying a high degree of nervousness and resistance to spontaneous disclosure of personal information. According to the available information, Wayne's difficulties had surfaced soon after his parents' divorce several years previously. Since the divorce, which was the culmination of a volatile marriage characterized by physical and emotional abuse of Wayne by the father, Wayne had had no friends and his school achievement had been sporadic.

As part of the evaluation, Wayne was requested to complete the RISB–H to assist in gathering information regarding his salient concerns. Several of the responses suggested that he was experiencing adjustment problems in a variety of areas.

The following completed sentences were typical of these concerns:

I regret *losing control of myself.*
I am very *happy, troubled, and confused.*
I feel *moderately relaxed and moderately agitated.*

These responses gave the examiner insight into many of the problems which were hindering Wayne's growth and development. During the clinical interview, Wayne admitted that he was bothered by thoughts of homicide and suicide. He portrayed himself as being critical, serious, and alone. His ambivalence toward his own abilities suggested that he was suffering from a poor self-concept and would require extensive individual psychotherapy. Additional data derived from other tests verified these initial hypotheses.

Thematic Apperception Test and Children's Apperception Test (TAT and CAT)

The Thematic Apperception Test (TAT) and a version for younger children, the Children's Apperception Test (CAT), are methods of determining dominant drives, emotions, and conflicts of an individual's personality.[12] The TAT was designed by Henry Murray, MD and his

Harvard colleagues in the early 1940s as an attempt to elicit underlying traits that an individual is usually not willing to disclose or of which he or she is unaware.[12] The CAT, developed by Leopold and Sonya Bellak in 1949, is often used with children from 3 to 10 years of age because of its reliance on animal pictures, with the TAT being administered thereafter.[13] A version of the CAT using humans (CAT–H) has also been developed for later latency and preadolescent children when the child appears too old for animal pictures yet too immature for adult situations as depicted in the TAT.[14] The apperception technique is viewed as being complementary to the Rorschach and is typically given along with the Rorschach during administration of the psychological battery to delineate more precisely areas of emotional conflict.

In this type of projective technique, the examinee is shown a series of ambiguous pictures of persons and scenes and is requested to make up stories about them. In creating these stories the examinee is asked to tell what led up to the situation portrayed in the picture, describe what the characters are thinking and feeling, and provide an ending to the story. The examinee is also encouraged to use his or her imagination and to relate whatever story first comes to mind. The procedure is intended to reveal basic themes that recur in a person's imaginative productions.

The TAT materials consist of 19 black and white pictures and one blank white card on which the examinee is instructed to create a completely novel event and relate a story about it. Although the original instructions suggested two one-hour sessions with ten cards presented during each session, most clinicians use an abridged set of about ten cards, choosing pictures which will probably elicit themes relating to the preferred problem areas, for example, depression.[15]

When interpreting TAT stories, the examiner attempts to determine the central character, or "hero" of the fictitious story, which is assumed to be the character with whom the examinee has identified. The subject matter of the stories is then analyzed in relation to Murray's consideration of "needs" and "press." Needs, in this regard, include such human characteristics as achievement, sex, aggression, and nurturance. Presses refer to environmental forces which may enhance or interfere with the satisfaction of needs. Being supported by friends when putting forth some effort or being exposed to parental arguments might be examples of presses. When deciding on the salience of a certain need or press, focus is directed toward the intensity, duration, and frequency of its occurrence across the stories. Unique associations are also assumed to have some significance for the person.

The word *apperception* also has meaning in the interpretation of stories. Apperception is a readiness to perceive in a manner based on previous personal experiences. Children often interpret the ambiguous pictures according to their own past experiences and invent stories in terms of preferred themes which reflect unique fantasies. If certain difficulties are troublesome to a child, they usually become evident within the organization of several stories. In analyzing responses to the TAT and CAT cards, the examiner looks for recurring themes or unusual responses which may reveal the individual's needs, motives, or characteristic manner of handling interpersonal relationships.

Although there is normative data which provides a global framework for interpreting TAT stories, most clinicians use personal intuition based on their own skills and experience to interpret a set of stories. The quantitative scoring systems and rating scales which have been constructed, although yielding good interrater reliability, are seldom used due to time constraints.[15] Thus, the objective use of the TAT is mostly left to research studies.

The CAT uses pictures of animals instead of people in the belief that young children can more easily identify with animals in storytelling productions.[13] The animals in the ten pictures of the CAT are depicted in various human situations, much like the anthropomorphic style in children's picture books. The pictures were designed to enhance comprehension of a child's important interpersonal relationships and his or her inner motivations. The pictures attempt to evoke fantasies associated with feeding problems, aggression, night fears, toilet training, acceptance, sibling rivalry, and attitudes toward parents as a couple and in relation to the child, for example, the oedipal complex.[13]

Like the TAT, the CAT focuses on the content of responses. Its main use is to delineate the factors which might be linked to the child's perceptions of himself or herself in peer groups, in school, or in the home situation. In this manner, the CAT becomes an important tool for the examiner, whether he or she be a psychologist or a psychologically trained physician. It can further be used in therapy as a play technique.

An analysis of the CAT requires a somewhat more varied approach than the traditional "theme" style of the TAT.[9 (p 145)] This is partly due to differences in cognitive development at different ages. For instance, simple descriptions of the pictures provided by an older child would seem defensive, whereas for children aged 4 to 7 this style of answering would provide some indication of normal intellectual development. Furthermore, attempts at interpreting young children's stories are also made difficult because of the stories' frequent brevity and lack of cohesiveness, thus making the detection of clear-cut themes a rarity.

The use of storytelling techniques, such as the TAT and CAT have always appealed to children and have been very popular with clinicians for some time. Their value comes mainly from the sensitivity and experience of the clinician rather than the particular stimulus material used.[16 (p 206)] For the less experienced clinician wanting to use the CAT and to be introduced to the TAT, Bellak's book[17] is an informative and instructive guide.

CASE ILLUSTRATIONS

The first card from the TAT series is a picture of a young boy contemplating a violin which rests on a table in front of him. It is considered an important picture for eliciting responses from the child concerning achievement motivation (a need) and also the types of environment conflicts (presses) the child is presently facing. The following responses show how this card may elicit these themes.

From an 11-year-old girl who appeared to be excessively anxious and unsure of receiving emotional support, particularly from maternal figures. Her ambivalence and indecisiveness toward a perceived lack of emotional support frequently intruded into her everyday interactions causing her to exhibit frequent mood swings and display highly demanding and clinging behaviors. This theme seemed to be central in the following story:

Once upon a time there was a little boy who knew how to play the violin. (Pause) One day his violin strings broke. (Pause) He tried so hard to fix them but it just wouldn't work, so the little boy sat down and looked at the fiddle and said to himself, "I wonder who could fix this?" (Pause) So he thought, "Maybe mom or dad can." (Pause) So he took it to mom and mom said, "Sure I can fix two of the strings," and then she went on with her own business. (Pause) Then he went to his dad and asked him if he could fix the rest of the strings. (Pause) Dad said, "Sure I can fix the strings." (Pause) So his dad fixed the strings and after that the little boy played his violin.

From a 12-year-old boy who was being evaluated because of a recent traumatic incident in his life. His sadness and insecurity were evident in the following story:

Little John had a violin. He would practice every day when he would have school practice the next day. (Pause) While everybody else was playing their violins, he just sat and thought about where he had left his notes. (Pause) He thought he was going to get in trouble for not getting the notes, but after all that worrying he found out that the teacher had extra notes. (Pause) After that day he never forgot his notes again and became a very good violin player. (Examiner: How did he feel?) Sad, because he thought he'd get in trouble.

From a 14-year-old girl with a WISC–R Verbal IQ of 62 who was being seen because of a suicide attempt. Her limited verbal skills and the shallowness of her emotions were apparent in the following story:

What is that, a violin? Once upon a time there was a boy playing violin and thinking, "Why should I play the violin because my schoolwork is terrible." (Examiner: How did he feel?) Down, he looks sad and mad. (Examiner: What happens next?) He goes off on somebody [i.e., gets in a fight] or he will talk [to someone]. (Pause) He's really hateful.

The Rorschach Technique

The Rorschach is the oldest and most widely used projective technique.[18] Hermann Rorschach began experimenting with inkblots in the second decade of this century. During the 1920s the Rorschach became popular in the United States and since then has spawned a large body of literature as well as considerable controversy regarding its use. In its current use it is assumed that the individual's responses to the problem-solving demands of the Rorschach are characteristic of his or her responses to more general problem-solving demands of the environment.

The Rorschach technique consists of ten standard inkblots printed on cards. Five are black and white and five make use of color. Responses are scored and interpreted to yield information about many personality and emotional variables including the individual's basic personality and coping style (deliberate and ideational as opposed to more immediate and affectively toned), style of thinking (e.g., simplistic and narrow, complex and ambitious), reality contact, degree of psychological distress, emotional reactivity, self-esteem, interpersonal relatedness, and more. The Rorschach is especially useful in clarifying diagnoses of major psychopathology including schizophrenia.

The Rorschach is individually administered by a highly trained examiner familiar with administration, scoring, and interpretation procedures. It is included as part of most psychological test batteries in virtually all settings in which psychologists perform evaluations. It can be administered to most any subject aged 3 years or older.

Through the years a number of systems have been developed for administering, scoring, and interpreting the Rorschach. Various approaches have been reviewed by Exner[19] who himself has developed the most thoroughly empirically based and psychometrically sound approach to the Rorschach, the Comprehensive System.[19,20,21] The following paragraphs draw on Exner's Comprehensive System.

The administration of the Rorschach involves a two-stage process. In the first part, the "free association," the cards are presented one at a time, in order, with the basic instruction, "Tell me what this looks like to you; what might it be?" Responses for each card are recorded verbatim as are any additional remarks or questions asked by the subject. The basic instructions and responses to the subject's questions are purposefully vague in order to provide a minimum amount of structure for the subject. Once all of the cards have been presented, the examiner conducts an "inquiry," going through the cards again in order to clarify and score the responses obtained in the free association. In the inquiry, the examiner is interested in determining which part(s) of the blot were used for each response and what it was about the blot that influenced the response.

Each response is scored for location (e.g., was the entire blot used or just a portion of it), determinant (was the response influenced by the contour of the blot, color, shading, movement, symmetry, etc.), and content area (human, animal, landscape, etc.). In addition, scores are noted for perceptual organizational sophistication, quality of form (does the percept match the contour of the blot), conventionality of the response, and the presence of thinking inefficiencies. All of these scores are recorded in special shorthand form.

The Comprehensive System makes use of a structural summary sheet that organizes and summarizes the various scores into a number of critical variables and ratios. It is from this structural summary that most of the interpretive hypotheses are derived. However, the sequence of responses and the actual content of the responses also are used in the interpretation.

Although other researchers have published developmental norms and special procedures for its use with children and adolescents,[22,23,24] the Comprehensive System has accomplished this more effectively and precisely. All of the critical variables, ratios, and special scores have been accumulated at yearly intervals from age 5 years through 16 years. At each year, from 5 to 16, data are based on from 105 to 150 individuals.

Historically, the Rorschach has been criticized for its low reliability and questionable validity.[25] However, the empirically strong base of the Comprehensive System has led to adequate test–retest reliability for most of the variables[19,20,21] as well as construct validity support for many of the personality interpretations.[19,20,21]

It should be noted that many clinicians employ the Rorschach in a more casual fashion, not making use of a formal system of scoring.[26] Although this use of the Rorschach as a semistructured interview increases the chances of subjective and possibly erroneous interpretations, it can enhance the clinician's feeling of understanding about the subject.[26] Like any other projective technique, the Rorschach provides information about an individual's personality but, as is also true for other projective techniques, other sources of personality information must be examined before firm conclusions can be made.

CASE ILLUSTRATION

Bob C. is a 14-year-old ninth-grader referred for a psychological evaluation by his guidance counselor because of increasingly disruptive behavior at school including fighting, destruction of property, and running through the girl's locker room. His grades, historically at a B and C level, had fallen to failing in virtually all subjects.

During the psychological assessment Bob was polite and cooperative. He could not account for his recent behavior problems but did discuss some family disruptions and said he was having problems getting along with his parents.

The results of the full psychological battery indicated average or better intellectual capabilities with mild to moderate variability among his verbal and nonverbal skills. Projective testing with the Rorschach showed considerable emotional turbulence. Unlike most youngsters his age, Bob did not evidence a consistent style of coping. Although he might make use of deliberate thinking strategies in problem-solving situations, he was just as likely to engage in poorly modulated, impulsive affective displays. This lack of a clearly defined personality style made Bob quite unpredictable. His available organized psychological resources were insufficient to manage his considerable inner distress. Influencing Bob's inner life were both long-standing feelings of dysphoria and more recently acquired distress including anxiety and feelings of helplessness.

With Bob's basically unpredictable response style, this emotional "overload" was interpreted as contributing to his acting-out behavior. Additionally, although not functioning with a formal thought disorder (i.e., a psychotic process), Bob was seen as experiencing some thinking inefficiencies, including an idiosyncratic "bending" of reality and uncritical thought processes. These thinking problems were seen as influencing his judgment and affecting his behavior.

From integration of these results with the other projective test data and information provided by Bob's parents, it was concluded that Bob's unacceptable behavior was one manifestation of his emotional disturbance. Long-standing depression and mounting family tensions were seen as important contributors to Bob's emotional difficulties. The psychologist recommended individual psychotherapy and family therapy along with consultation with school personnel in order to contain Bob's inappropriate behavior.

Minnesota Multiphasic Personality Inventory (MMPI)

The Minnesota Multiphasic Personality Inventory (MMPI) was originally organized in 1940 to provide an objective measure of certain major personality features which influence emotional and interpersonal adjustment. It was the first thoroughly empirical personality inventory.[27] The original scales (nine in all) were constructed for clinical use and named for the psychopathology on which the development was based. Unlike other personality tests of the time, the MMPI was not associated with theories concerning the organization of personality. Rather, it perpetuated the classification system derived from the work of Kraeplin, one of the pioneers of modern psychiatry. Although early criticism was directed at the lack of purity in item selection, much subsequent research has provided systematic and theoretical evidence for the validity of the selection.[28]

The MMPI belongs to that class of psychometric instruments which has been characterized as structured or of inventory type. This kind of instrument is usually presented in dichotomous form, that is, true–false, yes–no, agree–disagree, and the like. The MMPI itself consists of 566 statements that the individual is requested to answer as true or false, although there is a "cannot say" response that the person completing the form is encouraged to use only as necessary.

The MMPI currently consists of ten clinical scales and four validity scales, although additional experimental scales based on the MMPI are constantly being reported in the literature.[29] The ten clinical scales, which today are listed only by number to lessen the likelihood that excessive meaning might be attributed to their discarded clinical scale names (in parentheses), include: 1 (Hypochondriasis), 2 (Depression), 3 (Hysteria), 4 (Psychopathic Deviate), 5 (Masculine–Feminine), 6 (Paranoia), 7 (Psychasthenia), 8 (Schizophrenia), 9 (Hypomania), and 0 (Social Introversion). The validity scales are labeled: ? (Cannot say), L (Lie), F (Frequency), and K (Correction).[30] The function of the validity scales is to determine whether to accept the clinical profile with some degree of confidence or to indicate that much caution should be considered in interpreting the results.

The administration of the MMPI does not require the presence of someone specially trained in psychology and can be readily performed by ancillary medical personnel, aides, or receptionists. This flexibility in test administration is one of the most appealing features of the MMPI. The time that the test requires (typically between 1 and 1½ hours) is convenient to waiting periods in normal office practice and may provide the patient with additional confidence in the thoroughness and completeness of the clinician's examination. If the test is presented as a serious and important undertaking, the results should not be particularly influenced by the examining environment.

Because of its length, however, there have been numerous attempts to construct abbreviated forms of the test. The most acceptable shortened form includes only those items that are scored for the validity scales and clinical scales (399 items) and requires scoring modifications. The shortest form, the Mini-Mult, consisting of 71 items, has been utilized with nonreaders and can be orally administered.[30] However, the use of these short forms often leads to a loss of valuable information. Like all assessment measures, the MMPI at best is only a gross measure of pathology; reducing the number of items therefore impedes the overall reliability and validity of the instrument.

Scoring the MMPI and plotting the profile is relatively simple and can be done by the test administrator. When a large quantity of forms have been completed, the scoring sheets can also be sent off to a test scoring service. Interpretations, on the other hand, are complex and should be done only by persons trained in all of the scales' intricacies.[31] Over the last several years, there has been a burgeoning in "cookbook" interpretations and assorted computer-assisted interpretations. The major advantage of computerized interpretation is the speed involved in turnaround time. Whereas the clinician might spend over an hour in scoring and preparing the interpretation, the same operation by computer can be performed in seconds. It should be kept in mind that the use of these quick methods of interpretation do not constitute an adequate substitute for the clinical judgment process. If this interpretive route is necessary, the clinician should be thoroughly versed in the available service options.[28]

Although mainly used with adult populations, the MMPI is highly valuable in assessing emotional upheaval in adolescents, even down to the age of 12 or 13. It has been beneficial especially in predicting and understanding delinquency and school dropouts. A major caution in using the test with patients in their early teens is that a significant proportion of this age group demonstrates considerable discrepancy between verbal self-descriptions and actual behavior.

Although the MMPI Manual indicates that satisfactory results are obtained from individuals at least 16 years of age with a minimum of six years of schooling, experience suggests that properly motivated and carefully supervised persons with less than these minimum requirements are able to complete the forms successfully. Reading level seems to be the salient characteristic in taking this test. Two methods of quickly assessing the individual's capacity for understanding the test are to allow the individual to read aloud several of the items or to administer some brief measure of reading ability.

As noted earlier, when the test is administered to younger adolescents caution must be used in profile interpretation. Even if these youngsters can read well and are sufficiently motivated to complete the test, their range of experience is probably too limited to make the content of many items relevant to them. However, separate normative data for adolescents have been presented.[31]

Patients who are confused or who cannot understand the instructions can complete the test with alternative forms which have been constructed (e.g., individual cards instead of booklet form.[32] The availability of these separate forms ensures that the test can be administered to a broad spectrum of people. Besides the individual and group forms, researchers have developed forms for use with blind individuals or persons who cannot read the printed items, and for persons who have limited facility with the English language.

The MMPI seems also to be a favorite instrument in screening emotional problems in research populations. In recent years, investigations using the MMPI have focused on alcohol and drug abuse, parents of disturbed children, the development and validation of MMPI short forms, and the influence of race and age in MMPI interpretations.[29] More and more, the MMPI is being used extensively in medical patient research. These studies have encompassed three main areas: distinguishing psychogenic problems from organic disorders, specifying psychological factors associated with psychosomatic problems (e.g., asthma, ulcers), and predicting surgery outcome and rapidity of recovering from physical illness.

CASE ILLUSTRATION

John R., aged 15, was the only child of a couple who had adopted him shortly after birth. His natural mother was described as "uneducated, but energetic, healthy, and intelligent." His adoptive father,

63 years old, was a certified public accountant and was perceived by John as strict, old-fashioned, and critical. His adoptive mother, 58 years old, was an office supervisor for a church school board.

John was first seen by a psychologist in the first grade. This consultation was requested by his teacher who felt that John was bright but very unhappy. The psychologist at that time did not find enough concerns or symptoms to initiate treatment and did confirm above-average intelligence. John attended private schools through the eighth grade where he continually made poor grades and had numerous behavior problems. At John's request, he was placed in public school in the ninth grade but continued to barely pass. At that point, he reportedly became more hostile and negative toward his parents, at which time they requested assistance from the juvenile authorities. He was subsequently transferred to a vocational school where he failed the tenth grade due to absences. At the age of 15, John was placed in the custody of the state's juvenile services for driving without a license (wrecking his father's car) and repeated drug use.

A family physician in private practice provided medical care for the youngsters in the juvenile center in which John lived. This physician came to know John over the course of a year when she treated him for a variety of minor viral illnesses and one case of gonorrhea. The physician felt John was rather shallow and superficial in his dealings with her and other staff members, and she wanted to learn more about him in order to establish rapport and become more effectively involved with him.

She consulted with his counselors at the center and for additional information read through the psychological report on John's chart. One of the tests given during the assessment was the MMPI.

The particular standard or **T** scores, as derived from the raw scores, were:

1.	Hypochondriasis	52
2.	Depression	53
3.	Hysteria	54
4.	Psychopathic Deviate	79
5.	Masculine–Feminine	55
6.	Paranoia	59
7.	Psychasthenia	58
8.	Schizophrenia	60
9.	Hypomania	72
10.	Social Introversion	48

The validity scale scores were:

?	(Cannot say)	0
L	(Lie)	47
F	(Frequency)	62
K	(Correction)	46

The analysis of the MMPI profile in the report indicated that John had significantly high scores on scales 4 and 9. His validity scales did not show significant deviation from the mean, thus indicating the results to be a valid reflection of his current personality status at the time of testing. The report indicated that persons with a similar pattern of scores are usually immature, narcissistic, irritable, resentful, and flippant. They often use poor judgment and act without sufficient deliberation. They are generally evasive and attempt to handle problems through use of denial. Their attitude is negativistic and their rapport is basically superficial. They have difficulty in forming close emotional bonds with others and typically express many family problems. They are insecure and have great need for affection. Finally, the profile suggested an individual who was distractable and able to employ large amounts of energy, but whose enthusiasm concerning any particular matter is short-lived.

The physician who had been treating John medically felt that his profile conformed fairly accurately to her own impression of him in the brief time that she had seen him. She was not surprised to note that his profile suggested difficulties with interpersonal relationships and the likelihood of past family conflicts.

With the information provided by the MMPI and the remainder of the psychological report, as well as through her discussions with John's counselors at the center, she was able to amplify her own impressions of John and felt able to participate more actively at treatment team meetings.

References

1. Hammer EF: The Clinical Application of Projective Drawings. Springfield, Charles C Thomas, 1978.
2. Koppitz E: Psychological Evaluation of Children's Human Figure Drawings. New York, Grune & Stratton, 1967.
3. Goodenough F: Measurement of Intelligence by Drawings. New York, World Book Company, 1926.
4. Machover K: Personality Projection in the Drawing of a Human Figure. Springfield, Charles C Thomas, 1949.
5. Buck JN: The H–T–P technique, a quantitative and qualitative scoring method. J Clinical Psychology Monograph No. 5:1–120, 1948.
6. DiLeo JH: Child Development: Analysis and Synthesis. New York, Brunner/Mazel, 1977.
7. Rotter JB, Rafferty, JE: The Rotter Incomplete Sentences Blank. New York, Psychological Corp., 1950.
8. Rohde AR: The Sentence Completion Method: Its Diagnostic and Clinical Application to Mental Disorders. New York, Ronald, 1957.
9. Palmer JO: The Psychological Assessment of Children. New York, John Wiley, 1970.

10. Cofer CN: Review of the Rotter Incomplete Sentences Blank, in Buros OK (ed): *Fourth Mental Measurements Yearbook.* Highland Park, NJ, Gryphon Press, 1953, p 130.

11. Schofield W: Review of the Rotter Incomplete Sentences Blank, in Buros OK (ed): *Fourth Mental Measurements Yearbook.* Highland Park, NJ, Gryphon Press, 1953, p 131.

12. Murray HA: *Thematic Apperception Test.* Cambridge, MA, Harvard University Press, 1943.

13. Bellak L, Bellak S: *Children's Apperception Test.* New York, C.P.S. Co., 1949.

14. Bellak L, Bellak S: *A Human Version of the C.A.T.* New York, C.P.S. Co., 1965.

15. Anastasi A: *Psychological Testing, ed 2.* New York, Macmillan, 1961.

16. Wirt D: Review of the C.A.T., in Buros OK (ed): *Sixth Mental Measurements Yearbook.* Highland Park, NJ, Gryphon Press, 1965, p 206.

17. Bellak L: *The T.A.T. and C.A.T. in Clinical Use.* New York, Grune & Stratton Inc, 1971.

18. Rorschach H: *Rorschach Psychodiagnostic.* Bern, Switzerland, Hans Huber Medical Publisher, 1921.

19. Exner JE Jr: *The Rorschach: A Comprehensive System.* New York, John Wiley & Sons, 1974.

20. Exner JE Jr: *The Rorschach: A Comprehensive System, II: Current Research and Advanced Interpretations.* New York, John Wiley & Sons, 1978.

21. Exner JE Jr, Weiner IB: *The Rorschach: A Comprehensive System, III: Assessment of Children and Adolescents.* New York, John Wiley & Sons, 1982.

22. Halpern FA: *Clinical Approach to Children's Rorschachs.* New York, Grune & Stratton, 1953.

23. Ames LB, Metraux RW, Rodell JL, Walker RN: *Child Rorschach Responses: Developmental Trends from Two to Ten Years.* New York, Brunner/Mazel, 1974.

24. Ames LB, Metraux RW, Walker RN: *Adolescent Rorschach Responses: Developmental Trends from Ten to Sixteen Years.* New York, Brunner/Mazel, 1971.

25. Zubin J, Eron L, Schumer F: *An Experimental Approach to Projective Techniques.* New York, Wiley, 1965.

26. Aronow E, Reznikoff M: *Rorschach Content Interpretation.* New York, Grune & Stratton, 1976.

27. Hathaway SR, Meehl PE: *An Atlas for the Clinical Use of the MMPI.* Minneapolis, MN, University of Minnesota Press, 1952.

28. Alker HA: Review of the Minnesota Multiphasic Personality Inventory, in Buros OK (ed): *Eighth Mental Measurements Yearbook,* vol 1. Highland Park, New Jersey, Gryphon Press, 1978, p 931.

29. King GD: Review of the Minnesota Multiphasic Personality Inventory, in Buros OK (ed): *Eighth Mental Measurements Yearbook,* vol 1. Highland Park, NJ, Gryphon Press, 1978, p 935.

30. Hathaway SR, McKinley JC: *Minnesota Multiphasic Personality Inventory Manual,* rev. New York, Psychological Corporation, 1967.

31. Dahlstrom, WG, Welsh, CS, Dahlstrom, LE: *An MMPI Handbook,* rev ed, I, *Clinical Interpretation.* Minneapolis, MI, University of Minnesota Press, 1972.

32. Cottle WC: Card versus booklet forms for the MMPI. *J Applied Psychology* 34:255, 1950.

Chapter 12

The Relationship between Psychological Test Results and Medical and Neurological Problems

Psychological tests attempt to assess one or more of a variety of mental functions, including attention, memory, perception, cognitive abilities, language, mood, judgment, and thought content. Various medical and neurological problems of an acute and chronic nature may at times directly or indirectly affect these functions and thereby necessarily influence the results of psychological testing. Psychological testing in children on the other hand, although at times reflecting disordered biological functioning (here equated with "medical and neurological disorder"), is not of value in specifically diagnosing a particular medical condition, is of limited value in helping to localize the area of the brain affected by a particular lesion, and is usually superceded when precise localization is required for treatment purposes by better medical diagnostic aids such as X-ray studies. This chapter will clarify some of these relationships and provide examples of the interaction between medical problems and psychological test results.

The Effect of Transient Medical Problems on the Results of Psychological Testing

Children are often referred for psychological testing because of learning and/or behavior problems. The testing is invariably done at a scheduled time after the referral is made. If the child has an acute illness unrelated to the reason for referral, the testing—since it reflects mental processes at that particular time—may be affected and will not be a valid indicator of the child's general level of intellectual or emotional functioning. This situation can occur when previously healthy children with acute infectious diseases with fever or with severe pain because of trauma are seen for psychological testing. It can also theoretically occur with acute exacerbations of chronic illness (e.g., worsening respiratory problems in a child with previously stable cystic fibrosis).

CASE ILLUSTRATION

Melinda B., 3 years, 10 months old, was referred by her pediatrician for psychological testing because of general developmental delay of long standing. Birth history, growth parameters, and family history had all been negative. Testing with the Denver Developmental Screening Test (DDST) one month before had shown delays in gross motor, fine motor/adaptive, personal/social, and language areas. Behavior had not been a problem.

Melinda separated poorly from her mother for the testing session; she was irritable, uninterested, drowsy, and uncooperative. The psychologist guessed that Melinda might be experiencing separation anxiety and would be better motivated and more compliant with her mother present. This was only minimally helpful, however; and her mother agreed that Melinda was "not herself" and looked sick. She was not able to perform tasks (e.g., simple puzzles, drawing a circle, stacking blocks) that her mother assured the psychologist she could do at home.

The testing was stopped at this point and rescheduled. When Melinda arrived home her mother took her temperature; it was 39.4 degrees centigrade. She was later taken to a pediatrician who diagnosed an acute otitis media. Testing three weeks later was much improved in terms of attention, cooperation, effort, and results.

This case illustrates the obvious point that acute medical problems, often of a minor, self-limited nature, affect mental functioning adversely and render some results of psychological testing questionable. In these cases, the testing should be rescheduled.

The Effects of Chronic Medical Disorders on the Results of Psychological Testing

Children with chronic medical conditions whose primary organ or system of involvement is not the central nervous system are sometimes at risk for disordered psychological functioning relative to expectations based on their previous developmental or behavioral status or relative to the norm of functioning of other members of a comparable group without the chronic medical condition. This relationship has been studied more in terms of behavioral and emotional functioning than in terms of cognitive abilities.[1] Overall, it appears that children with physical disorders do have higher rates of emotional and behavioral problems than do control groups without medical disorders.[2] Studies specifically addressing changes in cognitive functioning in children with medical problems are, as noted, not numerous and crucial levels of severity when mental changes of a minor or subtle nature presumably occur, or the exact reasons why they might occur, are difficult to determine. Furthermore, it is difficult to determine whether poor test results in studies that have been done are due to specific deficits in cognitive or perceptual functioning or to disorders of attention or concentration which make valid psychological testing of specific cognitive skills difficult. Children with end-stage chronic renal disease[1] and iron deficiency anemia[3] are examples of patients in whom cognitive abilities seem to be impaired. In these cases, improved intellectual functioning has resulted after treatment. Children with congenital hypothyroidism on the other hand, have severe and irreversible intellectual deficiencies if not treated soon after birth.

The Effects of Known Neurological Disorders on Psychological Testing

Neurological disorders quite obviously produce alterations in learning and behavior and therefore may adversely affect the results of psychological testing.[4] The specific effects vary according to the extent of the neurological disorder, the site of the neurological disorder (although localization of function is not nearly so well established in children as it is in adults[4]), and, in the case of acute lesions, the time since the onset of the disorder. (Some recovery of function, for example, can often be expected with resolution of certain pathological processes such as cerebral edema or because other areas of the brain presumably can assume functions previously subserved by an injured area).

Psychological testing is valuable in many cases of disordered brain function not only to assess current behavioral and learning problems but also to monitor changes in these functions over time.

CASE ILLUSTRATION

Eva K., 2 years 9 months old, had been hospitalized three months prior to psychological testing because of the sudden onset of difficulty walking and inability to speak. Previous growth and development had been normal. At 2½ years of age she had been able to run well, peddle a tricycle and balance briefly on each foot. At that time Eva spoke using phrases, was able to say a few short sentences, and knew her first and last names.

One morning she awoke, stumbled out of bed, and fell. She screamed but could not respond to her mother's questions. Eva was evaluated neurologically and neuroradiographically. A number of laboratory tests were done. Eva was found to have suffered a cerebrovascular accident. A diagnosis of infantile hemiplegia was made. The pediatric neurologists felt she had suffered left cerebral hemisphere injury that included speech and language areas and motor cortex. She manifested cognitive impairment, language disorder, and motor deficits.

Eva subsequently regained some function over the next few months. She was nevertheless still markedly impaired at the time of psychological testing. Her gait was noticeably hemiparetic; she understood only the simplest of commands and was unable to vocalize any distinct words. She gestured with her left hand (mainly) when she wished to show others something or request an object.

Eva's pediatrician, working in conjunction with a multidisciplinary rehabilitation team which provided Eva with physical therapy, occupational therapy, speech and language therapy, and educational services, recommended that Eva have psychological testing to establish her current level of functioning and to serve as a baseline for future assessments. The testing employed a variety of scales including the Cattell Infant Intelligence Scale, the Stanford-Binet Intelligence Scale, and the Vineland Social Maturity Scale.

Although by history and developmental milestones, Eva's development had been within normal limits prior to her cerebrovascular accident, she now functioned at the upper end of the mildly mentally retarded range on the Stanford-Binet. She had an IQ of 65 and a mental age of 25 months. The psychologist noted that her language skills were more impaired than other cognitive functions, with receptive skills relatively better than expressive skills. On the Cattell Infant Intelligence Scale she had a mental age of 22 months and an IQ of 65. Her Social Age on the Vineland Social Maturity Scale was 21 months; this reflected both intellectual and motoric impairments.

The psychological report, which described Eva's test results did more than simply report the scores just cited. It discussed her approach to the test situation; her attempts to compensate for language, motor, and cognitive deficits; her particular strengths and weaknesses with a variety of test materials and situations; and her motivation, affect, and interpersonal skills. It offered some practical suggestions for working with her and suggested further that she receive an audiological evaluation which had not yet been done. Further testing to monitor changes over time was also recommended.

This case illustrates the value of psychological testing in defining more precisely the characteristics of a variety of mental functions that had been impaired by a neurological disorder. In the case presented, an acute alteration in mental functioning was discussed. Mental functioning of a variety of types (behavioral, cognitive, perceptual) is, of course, also assessed by psychological testing when the neurological disorder has been present on a chronic basis since birth or before (e.g., rubella syndrome, hypoxic brain damage due to birth trauma).

The case illustrates as well that psychological testing is the assessment of mental functioning at a particular point in time. Psychological testing makes no predictions about future functioning, nor does it make precise determinations about etiology.

Furthermore, on the basis of the psychological test results (as well as on the clinical examination) indicating that the child had sustained severe language impairment out of proportion to her other cognitive deficits, it would be appropriate to hypothesize that she probably had sustained injury to the language areas in the dominant hemisphere of the brain. This information, based on the psychological test results themselves, however, would have limited value if the child needed further medical intervention. Medical therapies (e.g., neurosurgical intervention if the child developed worsening function and an enlarging cystic lesion had to be ruled out) require evaluation aimed at the needs of the particular medical therapy contemplated (e.g., computerized axial tomography followed by angiography when surgery is considered) and are therefore addressed by diagnostic aids formulated specifically for these needs. Psychological testing may sometimes aid in localization in a general sense, but this localization is not adequate for biological therapies.

The Relationship Between "Organic" and "Functional" Brain Disorder. Further Comments on Psychological Testing as a Medical Diagnostic Aid

Psychologists and physicians have sometimes felt that when a particular child has a history indicating that neurological damage to the brain may have occurred (e.g., with birth trauma) and the child's psychological test results demonstrate specific deficits in functioning (e.g., perceptual motor difficulties), then that particular problem (say, the perceptual motor difficulties) is necessarily the result of the presumed neurological damage. Furthermore, for many years it was widely held that specific abnormalities on given tests (e.g., the Bender Visual Motor Gestalt Test)[5] nearly always meant that brain damage had occurred in that particular child.

Assuming children have "brain damage" solely because of findings on psychological tests would require specifically defining what particular findings on the psychological tests are being addressed, determining what types of alterations in brain structure or function are found on objective neurodiagnostic assessment in children who have suffered brain injury, and then correlating that particular psychological test abnormality with the known brain abnormalities. Even today research of this type is usually impractical or impossible.

"Neurological damage" itself, in fact, has frequently been defined by subjective physical neurological examination criteria and/or questionable histories suggesting that brain injury may have occurred. Psychological tests which are reputedly able to establish that brain damage has occurred on the basis of these kinds of imprecise medical evaluations are of questionable value, especially with regard to test findings for an individual child.

This caution about unverifiable assumptions of brain damage in children with no history (or weak history) suggesting brain damage not only applies to the older studies cited by Koppitz[5] in his discussion of abnormal findings on the Bender. It applies equally against assuming that children with abnormalities on the newer neuropsychological test batteries (see Chapter 9) have brain damage when there is no definite history or physical evidence suggesting it for a particular child.[6,7]

In our experience, the Bender has been used most often in making claims about brain damage in children. Koppitz,[8] the originator of the Developmental Bender Test Scoring System, in reviewing the uses of the Bender, comments that the test can generally reveal the presence of brain dysfunction in children but does not reveal the etiology of that dysfunction:[8]

Thus it is not possible to determine from a Bender Test protocol whether a youngster shows immaturity or malfunction in visual-motor perception as a result of a developmental lag or whether this is due to a genetic flaw or is the consequence of severe early deprivation or of brain trauma that resulted in a brain lesion. Additional information about the child's development and background and results from other tests are needed for a differential diagnosis.[8] (p 128)

Rutter further summarizes the situation in his review of the literature and concludes, "We still lack adequate tools with which to diagnose organic brain dysfunction when the clinical neurological examination is normal and when the history reveals no cause for brain injury."[6] (p 25) Various tests such as the newer neuropsychological test batteries, Rutter continues, can provide useful pointers to the possibility of brain injury but "they provide only circumstantial evidence, which is inadequate for individual diagnosis." Furthermore, there appears to be "no specific pattern of cognitive deficits that is diagnostic of brain injury."

In addition, it should be noted that in contrast to the situation in adults, in whom generally recognized behavioral syndromes (e.g., frontal lobe syndrome, temporal lobe syndrome) are associated with specific areas of brain dysfunction, severe brain damage in children is often related to emotional and behavioral problems, but there seems to be no association with the locus of injury and a particular emotional or behavioral problem.[4]

CASE ILLUSTRATION

Paul M. is 8 years, 4 months old and was referred for psychological testing by his third-grade teacher and by school administrators because of failing grades, severe academic problems, increasing frustration, and misbehavior in the academic environment.

On psychological testing, Paul's overall intelligence as assessed on the WISC–R was within the normal range; he had a 10-point Verbal–Performance discrepancy (not considered significant) and moderate subtest scatter. He demonstrated both distortions and rotational problems on the Bender Visual Motor Gestalt Test and his total number of errors on the Bender was more than one standard deviation above the mean for his age. On the Wide Range Achievement Test (WRAT), he functioned two years below expected grade level in reading and arithmetic and one year below expected grade level in spelling.

The psychologist concluded that Paul had a specific learning disability with impairment in visual-motor functioning (and perhaps

*in other areas also that were not specifically tested in that session).
These deficits were contributing to his academic weaknesses. Further educational testing was recommended to clarify more specifically the nature of the learning disability. The psychologist's report
noted that the findings on the Bender were suggestive of organic
damage, and he recommended a neurological evaluation and an
electroencephalogram (EEG).*

*Paul's mother, on hearing these recommendations, took Paul to
his pediatrician for clarification of the child's medical needs. The
pediatrician went over Paul's previous medical history and concluded that he had no past history of illness or disorder that is
known to cause brain damage. Physical examination also was normal. No dysmorphic features were noted. On careful neurological
examination, no hard neurological signs were noted. There were a
few "soft" signs such as awkwardness of finger opposition movements and slight choreiform movements on outstretched finger,[9]
but the significance of these are uncertain.[6]*

*The pediatrician concluded that Paul could not be said to have
definite evidence of brain damage on the basis of the psychological
test results or the finding of minor soft signs on neurological examination. He understood the considerations noted above and felt
that findings suggestive of organic damage on a psychological test
often rest on controversial research and that, in any case, an individual child who cannot be shown to have sustained neurological
damage by careful medical history and medical exam should not
be labeled as "brain-damaged." Paul certainly performed in an
abnormal manner statistically on the psychological tests and therefore could be said probably to have brain dysfunction of unknown
etiology.*

*Furthermore, a neurological evaluation beyond what had been
done by the careful primary care physician was not indicated and
probably would not be helpful therapeutically or diagnostically.
An EEG also was not indicated. There is considerable controversy
over the use of EEGs with children. Numerous minor, nonspecific
findings are often present in children's EEGs which some clinicians
would, and some clinicians would not, say indicate a brain abnormality.[6] Unless Paul had a suspected medical disorder such as
seizures for which an EEG would be indicated, the routine EEG
would not be helpful in diagnosing learning disabilities or in defin-
itively concluding that Paul's learning disability was due to organic
damage.*

*The pediatrician discussed his impressions with Paul's mother
and with Paul. He advised following the recommendations of the
psychologist for additional educational evaluation and treatment,
but felt no further medical evaluation was needed and that there*

was no definite evidence to suggest that Paul had been subject to brain damage in the past.

Several important points are clear from this and similar cases. Much of the confusion about the medical as opposed to the psychological and educational needs of a child results from confusion about terminology. The child in this illustration certainly appears to have a brain that functions differently from those of most children when confronted with a standard task on a psychological test. By definition, it seems satisfactory to say that he has *dysfunction*. But there is no evidence to say the child has had *damage* since this implies to many that an internal or external traumatic force has caused injury that results in the statistically deviant functioning. In an individual child there is often little evidence for this by the usual historical or physical criteria.

Another confusing term is *organic* as this is differentiated from *functional*. Many clinicians have traditionally felt that *organic* implies a known physical (usually structural) basis to a particular medical or psychological problem and that *functional* means that there is no physical basis to that particular problem. Implicit in this reasoning is the assumption that the child cannot help his or her dysfunction if it is organic but can change it if he or she wants to if the problem is functional, since the difficulty in this latter case is automatically *emotional*, hence not *real*. In fact, this reasoning is fallacious and often harmful since it encourages implicit criticism of children who have *functional disease*.

It is useful to assume in clinical work that mental processes, whether they do or do not deviate from accepted or statistical norms, or whether they are "normal" or "abnormal," reflect brain function that is organic in some sense. When particular tests, medical or psychological, show disordered functioning in one group of children and do not show disordered functioning in another group of children with the same clinical or educational problem (e.g., reading disabilities), the reason may lie with the particular test chosen and its inability to discriminate among children with the same or similar problems. In a related example, inability to demonstrate structural abnormalities in some children with a particular problem and ability to demonstrate structural abnormalities in other children with the same or similar appearing problem may reflect only the limits (in X-ray resolution, for example) of the test assessing the structural abnormality, or may indicate that the problem is not structural in all cases but rather at times pathophysiological (i.e., metabolic). To conclude, in these examples, that what can be demonstrated is "organic" and what cannot be demonstrated is "functional" (hence, "emotional") is not appropriate.

Another important consideration for physicians and child health care providers is the concern that psychologists frequently have as to whether children with signs of organic factors on psychological tests might have progressive medical disorders (e.g., tumors) that need medical referral and intervention. Earlier statements about organic indicators on psychological tests are important for the reader to review here.

In addition, it is important to mention that psychological testing would be likely to reflect disordered mental functioning as a result of brain tumor or other progressive disease processes at some point. It is not certain, however, that abnormal psychological test results would always precede the appearance of the better known signs and symptoms of medical disorders with brain pathology (e.g., headache, vomiting, diplopia, changes in observed behavior) that are used traditionally as diagnostic pointers in brain pathology. Clinically, questions about whether to institute additional medical tests to rule out disease processes rest on the history and physical examination. If learning or behavior problems have been present on a longstanding, chronic basis, and there are no new or significantly worsened problems in these areas, and if there are no signs or symptoms of disordered physical function (e.g., awkward movements, decreased appetite, headache, vomiting, staggering gait), there generally would be no further need for medical evaluation regardless of psychological test results. If a significant change in the character or severity of the learning or behavior problem has occurred in the recent past, or if signs or symptoms possibly suggestive of physical disorders are present (and especially if they have appeared recently), then a medical evaluation is certainly indicated. This, however, would have been true on the basis of any major change in the child's level of functioning behaviorally, cognitively, or physically, whether or not psychological testing had been done and regardless of what its results had been. In most cases then, it is the recent change in type or severity of a child's problems and/or the presence of traditional medical signs or symptoms that should cause referral to physicians for medical evaluation and not the findings on a psychological test.

References

1. Rasbury WC, Fennell RS III, Morris MK: Cognitive functioning of children with end-stage renal disease before and after successful transplantation. *J Pediatr* 102:589, 1983.

2. Rutter M, Tizard J, Yule M et al: Isle of Wight Studies, 1964–1974. *Psychological Medicine* 6:313, 1976.
3. Walter T, Kovalsky J, Stekel A: Effect of mild iron deficiency on infant mental development scores. *J Pediatr* 102:519, 1983.
4. Rutter M: Psychological sequelae of brain damage in children. *American Journal of Psychiatry* 138: 1533, 1981.
5. Koppitz, EM: *The Bender Gestalt Test for Young Children*. New York, Grune & Stratton, Inc, 1963.
6. Rutter M: Syndromes attributed to "minimal brain dysfunction" in children. *American Journal of Psychiatry* 139:21, 1982.
7. Boll TJ, Barth JT: Neuropsychology of brain damage in children, in Filskov SB, Boll TJ (eds): *Handbook of Clinical Neuropsychology*. New York, John Wiley & Sons, 1981.
8. Koppitz EM: *The Bender Gestalt Test for Young Children, vol II, Research and Application, 1963–1973*. New York, Grune & Stratton Inc, 1975.
9. Gabel S: The medical evaluation, in Gabel S and Erikson MT (eds): *Child Development and Developmental Disabilities*. Boston, Little, Brown & Co, 1980.

Chapter 13

The Child Health Professional Talks to Parents

THE INFORMING INTERVIEW

Parents may sometimes ask physicians and other child health care providers to obtain for their children's medical records the results of psychological tests performed in school or in a mental health clinic. At times the parents may want the clinician to explain the testing to them because they did not understand the initial interpretation when it was given or because they were too anxious to "hear" all that was said at that time. They may also want the physician to coordinate his or her services with those of the school or mental health provider.

At other times physicians themselves request psychological testing to help clarify or diagnose a particular learning or behavior problem as part of a more complete evaluation that may also include medical history, physical examination, other laboratory diagnostic aids, and possibly other consultants' opinions.

In both these cases, it is necessary for the health professional to inform the parents and, depending on developmental level and understanding, the child also, of the results of the evaluation of the child's problems, a major part of which has probably been the psychological testing.

The *informing interview* with the parents attempts to convey important information about the child's learning or behavior problems in a manner that reflects the physician's knowledge and thoroughness of approach on the one hand and his or her sensitivity and concern for the attitudes, feelings, and reactions of the parents and child on the other. The informing interview may also be a bridge between the child's difficulties in the past and his or her (and the family's) therapeutic involvement and more successful adaptation in the future. It must therefore serve as both an educational and motivational session for the parents, and perhaps as a therapeutic one as well.

These observations are true whether the child's problem is mental retardation, a specific learning disability, cerebral palsy with associated mental impairment, mild developmental delay, school behavior problems, common temper outbursts in a two-year-old, or any medical or psychological disorder of childhood.

Individual physicians and other child health care providers will approach this important session in their own unique style; it is therefore not appropriate to suggest a rigidly standard format for the session. Furthermore, the approach will vary not only with the particular clinician but also with the circumstances and the particular problem. The degree of stress in the session will also vary. Other things being equal, milder problems with less deviance on the part of the child from the parents' image of the ideal child will be more easily accepted by the parents, and the interview will be less stressful for them and for the physician. More severe problems that threaten the parents' values and ideals of what a child of theirs should be like will result in more parental stress, more physician stress, and a far more difficult interview.

There is relatively little said about the informing interview for parents of children with developmental problems in the medical literature.[1] Clinical experience and some reports[2] do support the notion that parents often feel that the timing of the session or the way it has been handled has not been helpful to them, however, and some parents appear to feel a good deal of anger toward the physician who has informed them of a serious problem. The literature that is available often considers the difficulties and disappointments in this informing session as a part of the broader problem of physicians' and parents' reactions to handicapped children. Much of the literature focuses on the parents' reactions when learning that their child is handicapped.[3] Parents frequently respond to this knowledge with a series of defensive reactions which include denial of the truth of the physician's diagnosis and prognosis; "shopping around" for other, more satisfying medical opinions; guilt feelings for what they may have done to cause the problem; anger and blame ascribed to themselves and to others who presumably are noncaring or negligent (such as physicians); shows of caring and concern for the child toward whom they may have hostility (reaction formation); and shame and embarrassment at their own inability to produce the child desired by them and by their society's values. Olshansky[4] has used the term "chronic sorrow" to reflect the ongoing grief of these parents who constantly mourn the loss of their ideal child and who unlike parents whose child has actually died of other causes cannot resolve their grief.

Finally, however, in some parents, a stage of more mature acceptance occurs. In this stage, the parents have a more adaptive reaction to their child and to his or her problem. They have accepted the child as a part of their lives and have adjusted well to their particular situation. If the clinician informing the parents expects the parents to be at this stage of mature acceptance when they are still at a stage of maladaptive defensiveness, confusion and failed communication between health care provider and parents will often result.[5]

Other authors have commented on physicians' reactions to handicapped children and how these reactions can affect the child's treatment and the physician's ability adequately to inform the parents of the problem and deal with their reactions. Physicians may feel frustrated and helpless in the face of a handicapped child; they may feel angry at the child, parents, or themselves because of their inability to cure the child and thus be what the concept of themselves as physicians requires. Physicians may withdraw from the parents in the face of their own anxiety about helplessness, incompetence, or dependency on others, or because of their own fears about mental disorder (a fear which they share with other members of the society). Nonpsychiatric physicians and other child health care providers may be unaccustomed to dealing with strong feelings in others and may feel inadequate or unable to comfort or support parents, or they may feel potentially overwhelmed by their own sadness and grief in the face of the handicapped child or by the parents' reactions to the child. Sometimes clinicians, knowingly or not, guard their feelings so carefully in these situations that they act and appear to be only intellectually involved; parents may later complain that the physician was cold, indifferent, or apathetic, and may express anger toward this "uncaring" approach.

It does not seem likely, however, that the frequent difficulties encountered in the informing interview can be accounted for solely on the basis of the maladaptive reactions of child health care providers or of parents. Jacobs[6] considers the problem of "information transfer" as contributing to poor communication in the informing interview session. Very little attention is given during medical training about how to convey medically important information. It is generally assumed that the clinician who is trained in taking a standard medical history, diagnosing illness, and treating disease will also competently communicate with parents in a manner that conveys information sensitively and adequately for the patient's needs. In fact, very little thought about how people learn, when they best attend to information that is presented, or how and when they remember what is presented to them has been applied in a formal manner in clinical medicine. It is probable that weaknesses in communicating cognitive information, along with the parents' and physicians' emotional reactions, are what make the informing interview with parents of children who have severe handicaps so often productive of anger, misunderstanding, and frustration.

Despite these difficulties in satisfactorily informing parents of their children's learning and behavior problems, successful informing interviews do occur. Some parents do make better adjustments to their child's problems than other parents do, perhaps partly because they have been properly informed. Or it may be that successfully adapting parents are psychologically better able to handle the information about their developmentally disabled or serverely disturbed child, but other factors probably also contribute. Some clinicians seem naturally more adept at effectively conveying information to parents than others. Those who are probably intuitively know when to repeat statements and how to use language appropriate to parental understandings that is neither misleading nor obscure. These physicians are better at emphasizing crucial information and avoiding digressions into less important areas; they probably understand the need to check the parents' understanding of what they have been told and the need to assess the level of parental sophistication at the outset so that information is conveyed on an appropriate level. These effective communicators are also probably adept at picking up verbal and nonverbal cues from parents indicating the latter's level of acceptance and coping ability. The effectively communicating clinician, in short, is aware of numerous factors that influence parents' understanding of information that is conveyed to them.

Clinicians who can communicate medical information effectively are probably able to respond well to the emotional reactions of the parents. It seems likely that this ability to respond to parental cues, to know when to slow down, when to repeat, and so on often involves the clinician's ability to relate to his or her own feelings when discussing a given child's severe developmental or behavioral problems.

Precise questions as to what attitudes and qualities some physicians possess that make patients respond to them positively, thus presumably enhancing their ability to successfully inform the parents, have rarely been addressed in a research sense,[7] although experienced clinicians agree on a number of important attitudes for physicians to convey to patients.[8]

In a clinical sense, patients (and parents) appear to respond to those who are able to convey through actions and manner that they will listen to what the parents are saying, try to understand their concerns in their own terms, pay attention to their fears, and spend the time necessary to know them and their situations better. Patients and parents respond to providers of health care who demonstrate that despite the hurried day, numerous other patients, possible confusion of scheduling, laboratory tests and bureaucratic procedures, they will know and remember them in a personal sense and will treat them in a concerned and confident manner as individuals.

The Informing Interview

Having considered particular qualities and characteristics of parents and providers that improve or hinder the chances of success in informing parents of their child's behavior or learning problems, we can now turn to the format of the informing session itself. First, it should be repeated that individual clinicians, particular situations, and particular types of problems all require flexible adjustments in format and approach. One general approach presented earlier[1] appears particularly well-suited to discussing severe developmental delays (e.g., mental retardation) with parents; it will be sketched briefly after the following case summary. Emphasis will be placed on a discussion of psychological testing during the informing interview. Another case, concerning a less severe disorder and utilizing a modified informing approach, will be presented subsequently.

CASE ILLUSTRATION

Audrey R. is 4 years, 2 months old and, along with her parents, has recently moved to the area. She is the only child of young parents and the product of the mother's first pregnancy. Generalized developmental delays have been noted since shortly after birth. Prenatal, perinatal, and subsequent medical history have all been unremarkable. Physical exam is normal; there are no dysmorphic features.

Audrey was seen by her new pediatrician for the first time a few months previously. Screening with the Denver Developmental

Screening Tests (on which she received several abnormal ratings), observation, and interaction with the child all made the pediatrician suspect that she was mentally retarded and functioning with a mental age of about two years. The mother said that Audrey had always been called "slow" but insisted that doctors had said she would "grow out of it." She was nevertheless quite worried, especially about Audrey's saying only short phrases, single words, and no sentences.

The pediatrician was unsure what had happened in discussions with other physicians in the past. He did not know if in fact former physicians had avoided discussing the child's developmental delays openly with the mother, why they had not evaluated her further etiologically, and why they had not obtained a more definite developmental assessment through psychological testing.

The pediatrician obtained previous medical records for Audrey, and when these confirmed the mother's statements about the lack of previous medical problems and the lack of evaluation for developmental delays he decided to evaluate the child further medically himself.[9] A decision was made to obtain psychological testing to confirm the suspected diagnosis, clarify strengths and weaknesses, aid in formulating a special education plan, and have a baseline for future testing. Psychological testing would also help him present the material to the parents in a more definitive manner during the informing interview.

The additional medical workup of chromosome studies and metabolic assessment revealed no etiology for Audrey's delays. Psychological testing showed her to have a mental age of 2 years 3 months on the Stanford-Binet and an IQ of 43, thus placing her in the moderately mentally retarded range. On the Vineland Scale for Social Maturity, she had a social quotient of 50, also in the mentally retarded range.

The informing interview with Audrey's parents might be structured along the following general lines, with the understanding that considerably more data (medical, social, family, psychological) should be available to the clinician at the time of the interview. More detailed information about the medical evaluation of the mentally retarded child is available elsewhere.[9]

Format of the Interview

Introductory Comments

Initially the clinician reviews pertinent aspects of the presenting problem as the parents have stated it. Then he makes a complimentary and true remark, for instance, "Audrey is a fine girl; I've enjoyed working with her." This emphasizes to the parents that others can like their child, that their child has positive qualities (which they often fear no one else will see), and that they have been (and can be) good parents.

Statement and Explanation of the Problem in Nonmedical Terms

In the case of a child with suspected severe developmental delays or mental retardation, the parents have been asked at some early stage in the examination to estimate how "old" they think their child is developmentally: "We know that Audrey is four years old; how old do you think she is in terms of what developmental skills she has, in terms of her development compared to other children her age?" At the inform-ing interview the clinician then states that the psychological testing showed the child to be functioning at whatever the correct mental age has been found to be. He or she then explains children's mental func-tioning in general and notes that some children are able to perform developmental tasks more or less ably than others and emphasizes where Audrey stands compared to other children.

Support for the Diagnosis of the Problem. Introduction of Medical Terms

The results of the psychological testing are discussed further. Psy-chological testing is described as a series of tasks or problems of dif-ferent types given to the child to do. It is explained that some tasks, depending on the child's age, involve using building blocks, putting puzzles together, trying to find a way through a maze, answering simple questions, doing arithmetic problems in writing or in one's head, defin-ing words, copying figures and the like. Many children have been given precisely the same tasks to do, and the psychologist compares how well one child does on these tasks with all other children of the same age who have taken the same tests. If a child does much better than average for his or her chronological age, the child is above average in what is called intelligence, which is really his or her ability to do the kinds of tasks on the test that give an indication of how well the child can learn things in life situations and in school. If a child does very poorly on the tests compared with others of the same age, we say that the child is mentally retarded. By that we mean that he or she is not able to learn as well as other children of that age and has not acquired as many developmental skills. The term *mental retardation* is just a description for a child who is not able to learn or understand things as well as other children of his or her age; the child will learn more in the future but will not catch up or learn as much as other children of the same age. Children who are mentally retarded, it can be stated, may be mildly, moderately, severely, or profoundly retarded.

The parents are then told their child, functioning at a particular mental age (which they may have approximated in their earlier reply to the question about their child's developmental age) therefore functions in the mentally retarded range. One may add, if possible, a softener by saying (in the case presented) that the child is in the moderate but not severe range of mental retardation ("Audrey is a moderately retarded child. She is not a profoundly retarded child.") The clinician might also add, "In using the words *mentally retarded* to describe Audrey we are really using a term to describe her developmental abilities which corresponds pretty well with what you yourself have told us when you said she was able to perform activities, function, and learn as much as a child who is two years old."

It should be noted here that any medical or nonmedical terms likely to have an emotional impact on parents (e.g., mental retardation, brain damage) should be carefully explained in sensitive, straightforward, simple terms that attempt to demystify the frightening words (e.g., the above explanation of mental retardation). Diagrams or charts may be helpful to illustrate or clarify.

Results of Further Medical Tests and Discussion of Etiology

Repeated here, according to the parental level of understanding, are the tests performed, why they were done, and whether any etiological statement is possible ("The results of Audrey's blood test and urine test show no definite cause for her problems in development").

Discussion of Further Questions

As an aid in conceptualizing and remembering the problems and needs of parents in the informing interview, it is sometimes helpful to think in terms of answering stated and unstated questions the parents may have that have not yet been addressed: (1) What direct questions have been asked? (2) What questions are *really* being asked? (3) What questions are *not* being asked? (4) What questions *should* be asked?"[1] (p 234)

In this formulation the clinician is reminded to address, within the limits of parental understanding at that time, the parents' additional *stated* concerns (e.g., responding to the mother's initial question of why Audrey is still not talking as a function of her mental retardation).

The clinician then articulates and "answers" the anxiety-raising questions the parents probably will be afraid to ask: Will she be able to go to regular school? Will she ever talk more? Will she be able to care for herself?

The clinician then phrases and discusses the questions that fear and guilt will doubtless raise in the parents' minds: Did I (we) do anything wrong? Could this have been prevented if I hadn't been so upset during the pregnancy, or had eaten less, or hadn't had that cocktail every night before dinner? Will she be able to marry, have children, live outside the home?

The clinician may wish to address practical questions that concern future management or additional study. Medication, schooling, special therapy needs, additional consultation, inpatient treatment if needed for control of seizures, and so forth may all be addressed if they have not been discussed previously.

In answering the unasked questions the clinician does not generally ask the parents directly whether they are worried that their child will not talk, or will not be able to marry, or whether they have personal guilt unless these queries are quite close to the surface and strongly implied by the parents themselves. More often the clinician will say, "I get the feeling you may be concerned that Audrey will not be able to care for herself when she begins menstruating" and then lets the parents respond accordingly. Quite often the clinician, from a knowledge of parents of developmentally handicapped children in general and of the present parents in particular, will suggest answers to unvoiced questions (that are within the range of parental coping ability) in an unassuming, nonthreatening manner: "Parents often wonder if children like Audrey who are mentally retarded will be able to live on their own later on." The clinician then waits a moment to see the parental response, if any, and proceeds to clarify or answer the question as appropriate. Or, "Parents with mentally retarded children often feel that their child wouldn't be mentally retarded if they had done something differently." The clinician waits for a response; if none is forthcoming, he reassures the parents (if at all possible based on the information available): "There was nothing that we know of that either of you could have done differently to have changed the outcome or to have helped Audrey in any other way. This seems to have been just a random happening—a random distribution of the genes [a term that may need explanation]—at the time of conception." (A discussion of the likelihood of recurrence genetically is almost always important, and the clinician may advise further genetic consultation at the appropriate time.)

Response from Parents: Eliciting Comments and Questions

The clinician emphasizes that he wants to answer any questions the parents may have. He may add that he is unsure of what needs to be repeated, what he might have neglected to say, or what needs clarification. He may further ask the parents to explain what they have understood to have been said to them thus far in the session. The parents' response should help to assess their understanding and show the clinician what needs reemphasis or what the parents have been unable to accept emotionally.[1,10]

Plans for Followup and Future Contacts

The date and time of next contact with the physician for counseling or additional informing is scheduled. Notification is given that the clinician himself or another staff member will be calling the parents in a week or so to see if they have further questions (actually to see how they are doing emotionally and if they have followed through on scheduled appointments and so on).

Approval of Parents' Efforts

The clinician commends the parents' judgment in having the child evaluated, thereby trying to support their self-perception as good, caring parents, and motivate them further to obtain future services for the child. The session is closed, perhaps with a comment that the clinician will look forward to getting a copy of the consultant's report (if this is suggested) and will look forward to seeing them and the child at the next meeting.

CASE ILLUSTRATION

Jessie P. is 8 years, 3 months old and is currently in the fourth grade. He has been followed by the same physician for the last five years. Medical history prior to that time, and since age 3, has been unremarkable. Development has been normal. He is an only child.

Until six months or so previously, adjustment had been good. No behavior problems were present in home or school environments. In the last several months, however, academic work in school has deteriorated from a previously above-average level; the teacher has reported that he is "always into something," overactive, distractable, frequently fighting with peers. The mother, who brought Jessie in for evaluation, also notes the change over the last several months, with constant fighting, nervousness, oppositional behavior, and moodiness. She wonders if he is "hyperactive" and whether he needs something to "quiet him down." Additional history shows that the parents separated shortly before Jessie's problems became apparent. Contact is maintained with the father and Jessie stays with the father on weekends. He has experienced no major medical problems during the time of his deteriorating academic work and behavioral difficulties, although he has occasional headaches.

The evaluation by Jessie's physician consisted of two interview and play sessions, a physical exam, one interview with the mother (the father declined to come for an interview, saying he could not get away from work), a conversation by phone with the teacher after obtaining parental permission (and discussing this with Jessie), and the recommendation for psychological testing. The latter was advised after the physician had completed his own evaluation. He felt Jessie was probably having difficulties adjusting to the recent marital discord and separation and that his behavioral deterioration and school problems reflected these difficulties. Nevertheless, he decided to recommend psychological testing for a number of reasons. Jessie was showing academic deterioration and a current assessment of intellectual functioning would be helpful. In addition, a second opinion about Jessie's behavior problems and projective testing to supplement the clinician's own impressions would be helpful in subsequent work with the boy and his parent(s). Furthermore, although the pediatrician felt that Jessie's history and findings were not that of a child with an attention deficit disorder, he sensed the mother's anxiety about the term hyperactivity and thought that an additional opinion about this issue through psychological testing might be reassuring to her.

After the physician's own evaluation was finished and the psychological testing had been completed by a colleague with whom he discussed the case personally, the clinician held an informing interview with the mother. The format outlined in Audrey's case could still have been followed in a general sense, but this child's generally good functioning, less severe problem, good prognosis, and small likelihood of severe parental reaction of guilt, loss, or helplessness made the clinician less concerned with severe anxiety or the need to answer those unspoken questions of the prior case. In this case, the need to enhance parental self-esteem, provide support for the parents in their grief, state the probability of long-term agency or school involvement are not the prominent concerns they were in the previous example. A brief review of this type of session follows, with an emphasis on the physician's explanation of the psychological testing.

The physician will at the outset try to convey an informal, supportive, concerned attitude. He will outline the problem, using as much of the parents' own statements as possible: "Mrs. P., you mentioned when you brought Jessie in that he was having behavior problems in school; his grades were falling; he was having behavior problems at home too; and you wondered if he was hyperactive and needed medication."

The clinician's explanation of what the problem is and how he or she came to that conclusion will follow: "After you and I spoke together in our session and you mentioned your difficult marital separation and the family problems you all experienced even before that, I wanted to check the extent to which the home environment might be contributing to Jessie's school difficulties and behavioral problems. When I saw him alone those few times we talked a good deal about his reactions to the separation, how he felt nervous and confused a lot now, and how he was also sad. He is an intelligent boy and quite verbal, and after we established some rapport he was pretty open, even in just those two sessions. We also played some games, and he drew some pictures for me. The pictures and games children draw and play tell a lot about them that they're not always aware of or can't easily verbalize. I asked Jessie to draw a picture of a person, and after he did this, I asked him some questions about the boy he had drawn and I also asked him to tell me a story about the boy he drew. I got the feeling from the drawing he did and the story he told that he really was feeling sad and also angry and frightened these days." (See Chapters 11 and 12 for discussions of children's drawings and how they may be used in the assessment of developmental and behavior problems.)

The physician might continue, "I didn't think Jessie was hyperactive during the time I saw him or after I spoke to his teacher and reviewed his medical history. A truly hyperactive child will be that way from birth or shortly thereafter. Jessie is fidgety now because he is nervous and not because of a basic hyperactive behavior pattern. I also don't think Jessie has specific learning problems because he has done well in school before this year and because there has been no family history of learning problems; but because his school work has deteriorated, and there was some question of hyperactivity, I wanted another opinion about Jessie and his emotional functioning so I advised the psychological testing that he had last week."

Here the clinician might go through what psychological testing is, as in the previous example, perhaps giving age-appropriate arithmetic problems, vocabulary words, forms and figures to be copied (that are not, however, identical to test items) as examples of the type of test items to which the child might be exposed. The clinician would explain the child's results on the testing ("Jessie's overall intelligence is above average; he is slightly ahead of grade level in reading; there were no significant areas in which he was weak in terms of his learning abilities"). Emphasis here also might be drawn to the fact that hyperactive children frequently show characteristic patterns on psychological testing (e.g., the distractability factor, subtest scatter; see Chapter 7) and that Jessie did not have problems in those areas. The clinician might then mention that the psychologist felt, as he himself did, that Jessie's school problems and failing grades were because of his inability to concentrate in school at this time. This itself was because he was emotionally upset, anxious and sad a good deal of the time since the problems between his parents had surfaced.

At this point, if appropriate, the clinician might discuss the rest of the testing and describe what projective testing is and how other projective tests, like the drawings he himself had Jessie do, help a child to show his or her problems, reactions, attitudes, and characteristics even if the child does not realize that these reactions and attitudes (his or her "feelings") are there. The clinician might then go over the psychologist's comments on the stories Jessie made up on the Children's Apperception Test and perhaps even give an example to illustrate the boy's confusion of loyalties between the parents, possible feelings of guilt about his presumption that he caused the marriage to fail, anger toward one parent or another, feelings of being helpless, and so on.

Depending on circumstances, the clinician might then explain one of the drawings Jessie had made during the clinician's own assessment to the parent and describe some of the comments that he had made in a general way to illustrate the emotional reactions the boy was experiencing. The clinician might also comment on the psychologist's report and the latter's view of how Jessie experienced himself through his drawings and stories. Again, these would be tied to Jessie's current reactions and problems as the mother understands them.

Next the clinician might mention that from what the mother has told him, she herself has been having some difficulties since the separation, and has realized (if she has) that her own reactions have had an impact on Jessie, just as his behavior and reactions have affected her. It would be mentioned that she herself could benefit from ongoing therapy sessions which would involve talking about Jessie, his problems and needs, and also discussing to some extent her own needs and reactions in this understandably stressful period.

In most cases questions by the parents should be encouraged throughout the informing session and the clinician might pause to ask if there are any at this point.

Specific recommendations for further therapy should be discussed with the parents. The clinician here, depending on time, experience, and ability, may feel comfortable in providing a series of therapy sessions for the child himself. In this case, the mother may be seen by the same clinician or by a social worker or psychologist with whom the clinician can coordinate efforts.[13,14] Alternatively, the child and parent can be referred for therapy elsewhere.

The mother should be told that if possible the father be informed and also involved in the therapy and that the clinician is willing to report the findings to him as well. The child, in this example, should also have the benefit of an informing session since his understanding is certainly sufficient (unlike the child in the previous example who probably would not benefit). If it is decided that the same clinician will be seeing the child in therapy, the results of the assessment can merge with the first therapy session. The clinician should also either ask the mother to have the teacher call or call the teacher himself and discuss Jessie's problems and management (after mentioning to Jessie that he thinks this is a good idea and, in a general way, mentioning what will be said).

With psychotherapy arrangements having been discussed, further questions might again be encouraged. Lastly, scheduling for subsequent sessions or contacts is made with a positive or encouraging comment, if at all possible: "It's good you brought Jessie in; both you and he seem to have been having a hard time recently, and I think now you will be able to begin sorting things out. I hope you and Jessie will be feeling better soon."

References

1. Gabel S: The informing interview, in Gabel S and Erickson MT (eds): *Child Development and Developmental Disabilities.* Boston, Little, Brown & Co, 1980.
2. Giannini MJ: The role of the physician in mental retardation. *Journal of the American Medical Women's Association* 24:491, 1969.
3. Group for the Advancement of Psychiatry: *Mental Retardation: A Family Crisis— The Therapeutic Role of the Physician.* Report No. 56. New York, 1963.

4. Olshensky S: Chronic sorrow: *Response to having a mentally defective child*. Social Casework 43:190, 1962.
5. Miller LG: Toward a greater understanding of the parents of the mentally retarded child. *J Pediatr* 73:700, 1968.
6. Jacobs J: Perplexity, confusion, and suspicion: A study of selected forms of doctor–patient interactions. *Social Science and Medicine* 5:157, 1971.
7. Nicholi AM Jr: The therapist–patient relationship, in Nicholi AM Jr (ed): *The Harvard Guide to Modern Psychiatry*. Cambridge, Belknap Press of Harvard University Press, 1978.
8. Gabel S: The general assessment, in Gabel S (ed): *Behavioral Problems in Childhood: A Primary Care Approach*. New York, Grune & Stratton, Inc, 1981.
9. Gabel S: The medical evaluation, in Gabel S and Erickson MT (eds): *Child Development and Developmental Disabilities*. Boston, Little, Brown & Co, 1980.
10. Selig AL: Common myths of family feedback conferences. *Journal of Developmental and Behavioral Pediatrics* 4:67, 1983.
11. Harris DB: *Children's Drawings as Measures of Intellectual Maturity*. New York, Harcourt, Brace & World, 1963.
12. Koppitz E: *Psychological Evaluation of Children's Human Figure Drawings*. New York, Grune & Stratton Inc, 1967.
13. Townsend EH Jr: The social worker in pediatric practice. *Am J Dis Child* 107:77, 1964.
14. Gabel S: The primary health care provider's role in the provision of mental health services and the prevention of mental illness in children, in Gabel S (ed): *Behavioral Problems in Childhood: A Primary Care Approach*. Grune & Stratton, Inc, 1981.

Index

Age level
  Bender Visual Motor Gestalt Test, 102
  Halstead-Reitan Batteries, 111
  Illinois Test of Psycholinguistic Abilities, 94
  Kaufman Assessment Battery for Children, 84
  Leiter International Performance Scale, 89
  Luria-Nebraska Children's Battery, 117
  McCarthy Scales of Children's Abilities, 82
  norms and, 3–4
  Stanford-Binet Intelligence Scale, 70–71
  Wechsler Scales, 76
  Wide Range Achievement Test, 99
Agreement. See Interrater agreement
American Association on Mental Deficiency, 121, 122–24
Assessment. See Tests and testing; entries under names of specific tests

Bayley Scales of Infant Development, 66–69
Behavior Problem Checklist, 46
Behavior problems
  physical illness and, 154
  physicians and, 10–17

Behavior problems (Cont.)
  psychological report and, 26–27
Behavior rating scales, 35–47
  Behavior Problem Checklist, 46
  cautions in use of, 35–36
  Child Behavior Checklist/Revised
    Child Behavior Profile, 37–46
  Conners' Teacher Rating Scale/Parent's Questionnaire, 36–37
  types of, 35
Bender Visual Motor Gestalt Test, 101–105, 158
Brain damage
  Halstead-Reitan Batteries, 114–115
  testing and, 155–157, 158–162

Child Behavior Checklist, 37–41
Children's Apperception Test (CAT), 139–143
Client-therapist relationship, 6
Clinical problems, 5–6
Cognitive measures, 65–92
  Bayley Scales of Infant Development, 66–69
  Kaufman Assessment Battery for Children, 84–91
  Leiter International Performance Scale, 89–91
  McCarthy Scales of Children's Abilities, 82–84
  purposes of, 65

181

Cognitive measures (*Cont.*)
    requirements of, 65
    Stanford-Binet Intelligence Scale, 69–
        75
    Wechsler Scales (WISC-R & WPPSI),
        75–81
Conners' Parent's Questionnaire, 36–37
Conners' Teacher Rating Scale, 36–37

Data collection, 26–27
Demographics, 26
Denver Developmental Screening Test
    (DDST), 49, 50–54
Developmental Screening Inventory
    (DSI), 49, 54–55
Developmental Test of Visual Motor
    Integration (VMI), 105–106
*Diagnostic and Statistical Manual of
    Mental Disorders* (DSM-III), 121–
    122
Draw-A-Person Test (Goodenough-Har-
    ris Drawing Test), 49, 55–58,
    130–131

Educational/perceptual testing, 93–107
    Bender Visual Motor Gestalt Test,
        101–105
    Developmental Test of Visual Motor
        Integration, 105–106
    Illinois Test of Psycholinguistic Abili-
        ties, 94–96
    Peabody Individual Achievement
        Test, 96–99
    purposes of, 93
    Wide Range Achievement Test, 99–
        101
Education for All Handicapped Chil-
    dren Act, 122
Electroencephalography, 160
Errors, 4

Family
    psychological report and, 26
    referral and, 20
    See also Informing interview
Family drawing, 130–137

Goodenough-Harris Drawing Test
    (Draw-A-Person Test), 49, 55–58

Halstead-Reitan Neuropsychological
    Test Batteries for Children, 110–
    116
History. *See* Patient history
House-Tree-Person drawing, 130–137
Human Figure Drawing (Goodenough-
    Harris Drawing Test), 49, 55–58
Hyperactivity, 36–37

Illinois Test of Psycholinguistic Abili-
    ties (ITPA), 94–96
Individual differences, 3
Informing interview, 165–179
    case example of, 169–170, 174–178
    effective, 168–169
    format of, 170–174
    information on, 166–167
    information transfer and, 167–168
    physician reaction and, 167
    purposes of, 165–166
Insurance, 21
Intelligence
    norms and, 3
    social/adaptive skills tests and, 121
Intelligence tests. *See* Cognitive
    measures
Interrater agreement, 35–36
Interview. *See* Informing interview

Kaufman Assessment Battery for Chil-
    dren (K-ABC), 84–89

Learning disorders
    physical illness and, 154
    physicians and, 10–17
Leiter International Performance Scale,
    89–91
Licensure, 22
Luria-Nebraska Children's Battery, 117–
    119

McCarthy Scales of Children's Abilities,
    82–84
Medical problems. *See* Physical illness
Mental retardation, 122
Minnesota Multiphasic Personality
    Inventory (MMPI), 146–150

Neurological disorders
testing and, 155–157
See also Physical illness
Neuropsychological tests, 109–119
Halstead-Reitan Neuropsychological
Test Batteries for Children, 110–
116
Luria-Nebraska Children's Battery,
117–119
purposes of, 109
referral and, 110
Norms, 3

Objectivity, 4

Parents. See Family
Patient history, 23–24
Peabody Individual Achievement Test
(PIAT), 96–99
Peabody Picture Vocabulary Test-
Revised (PPVT-R), 49, 58–61
Perceptual testing. See Educational/per-
ceptual testing
Personality inventories, 129–151
Minnesota Multiphasic Personality
Inventory (MMPI), 146–150
overview of, 129–130
projective drawings, 130–137
Rorschach technique, 143–146
sentence completion tests, 137–139
Thematic Apperception Test (TAT)
and Children's Apperception
Test (CAT), 139–143
Physical illness, 153–163
brain disorder, 158–162
chronic medical problems, 155
neurological disorders, 155–157
transient medical problems, 154
Physicians, 9–18
informing interview and, 165–166
psychologist selection by, 19–22
reactions of, 167
referrals by, 12–17
testing expertise of, 22–23
testing performed by, 10–12
Primary care physicians. See Physicians
Projective drawings, 130–137
Projective measures. See Personality
inventories
Psycholinguistic age score (PLA), 95

Psychological report, 25–33
analysis/interpretation, 27
areas of, 25
case history, 26
data and observations, 26–27
demographic information, 26
example of, 27–33
listing of tests and results, 26
narrative portion, 27
testing history, 26
Psychological specialties, 21–22
Psychological testing. See Tests and
testing

Qualifications (psychologists'), 22
Quay–Peterson Behavior Problem
Checklist, 46

Referral, 19–24
making of, 23–24
neuropsychological tests, 110
physicians, 12–17
psychological report and, 25–33
psychologist selection and, 19–22
testing expertise and, 22–23
test selection and, 4
Revised Child Behavior Profile, 37, 42–
45
Rorschach technique, 143–146
Rorschach Test, 130
Rotter Incomplete Sentences Blank-
High School Form (RISB-H), 138–
139

Schools, 20–21
Screening instruments, 49–63
Denver Developmental Screening
Test, 50–54
Developmental Screening Inventory,
50–54
examples of, 49
Goodenough-Harris Drawing Test
(Draw-A-Person Test), 55–58
Peabody Picture Vocabulary Test–
Revised, 58–61
purposes of, 49
Slosson Intelligence Test, 61–62
Sentence completion tests, 137–139
Slosson Intelligence Test, 49, 61–62

Social-adaptive skills tests, 121–127
  American Association on Mental
    Deficiency Adaptive Behavior
    Scale, 122–124
  overview of, 121–122
  Vineland Social Maturity Scale and
    Vineland Adaptive Behavior
    Scales, 124–127
Stanford-Binet Intelligence Scale, 69–75

Test results, 26
Tests and testing
  age level and, 3–4
  brain disorder and, 158–162
  chronic medical disorders and, 155
  clinical problems and, 5–6
  defined, 3
  error and, 4
  individual differences and, 3
  medical/neurological problems and,
    153–163
  need for, 1–3

Tests and testing (*Cont.*)
  norms and, 3
  physicians and, 10–12
  psychological report and, 25–33
  psychologist role in, 6
  referral for, 19–24
  selection of test, 4–5
  transient medical problems and, 154
  See also entries under names of spe-
    cific tests
Thematic Apperception Test (TAT),
  139–143, 154
Treatment, 2

Vineland Adaptive Behavior Scale,
  124–127
Vineland Social Maturity Scale, 124–
  127

Wechsler Scales (WISC-R & WPPSI),
  75–81
Wide Range Achievement Test (WRAT),
  99–101